FULL ASSURANCE

FULL ASSURANCE

H. A. IRONSIDE

MOODY PRESS ● CHICAGO

Printed in the United States of America

CONTENTS

CONTENTS

INTRODUCTION

IN PENNING the following pages, I have had but one outstanding object before me—to make as plain as I possibly can just how any troubled soul may find settled peace with God. I am thinking particularly of those people who believe the Holy Scriptures to be divinely inspired, and who recognize that salvation is only to be found in Christ, but someway have missed the "peace of a perfect trust," and though earnestly desiring to know the Lord, are floundering in perplexity of mind, like Bunyan's pilgrim, in the Slough of Despond, or like the same anxious inquirer in his earlier experience, trembling beneath the frowning cliffs of Sinai.

Consequently, no attempt is here made to prove that the Bible is true, as both the writer and the readers he has specially in view take that for granted. People who are bothered by doubts along that line may find abundant help elsewhere, as there are not wanting plenty of good books, written by sound Christian scholars, that present unanswerable arguments for the inerrancy and the divine authority of the Bible. The trouble is that so many people who profess to want help along these lines are too indifferent to investigate, even when the opportunity is put before them. It is of really earnest seekers after the truth that I am thinking.

For many months I was myself in much doubt and confusion of thought until God by His Holy Spirit showed me through His Word the true ground of peace. That was many years ago, and as I write I find myself living over again the conflict of those days, and recalling, as though it were but yesterday, the gladness that filled my soul when I rested in Christ alone, and entered into a lasting peace with God that has known no disturbance throughout the years.

The clouds may at times veil my sky. Sorrows and difficulties may try my soul. New discoveries of the corruption of my own heart may bring humiliation and repentance. But this peace with God remains unchanged, for it rests not on me, not on my frames of mind or experiences, but on the finished work of Christ and the testimony of the Word of God, of which it is written: "For ever, O Lord, thy word is settled in heaven."

PART I

1

STRIVINGS AFTER ASSURANCE

IN A MINISTRY of almost half a century, I have had the joy of leading many to rest in Christ. And I have found that the questions that perplex and the hindrances to full assurance are all more or less basically alike, though expressed differently by different people. So I have sought in this little volume to set forth, as clearly as I know how, the truths that I have proved basic in meeting the needs of thousands of souls.

I have been told that in days gone by young doctors were in the habit of using a great number of medicines in their endeavors to help their various patients, but that with increasing practice and larger experience, they discarded many remedies which they found were of little use and thereafter concentrated on a few that they had proven to be really worthwhile.

The physician of souls is likely to have much the same experience, and while this may give a somewhat uninteresting sameness to his later ministrations, as compared or contrasted with his earlier ones, it puts him after all in the immediate succession of the apostles of our Lord, whose viewpoint may be summed up in words written by the greatest of them all: "I determined not to know anything among you, save Jesus Christ, and him crucified." Here is the sovereign remedy for all spiritual ills. Here is the one supreme message that is needed, whether they realize it or not, by all men everywhere. And this I have tried to proclaim in these unpretending pages.

As an Itinerant Preacher

For the most of my life I have been an itinerant preacher of the gospel, traveling often as much as thirty to forty thousand miles a year to proclaim the unsearchable riches of Christ. In all these years I only recall two occasions on which I have missed my trains. One was by becoming confused between what is known as daylight saving and standard time. The other was through the passive assurance of a farmer-host, who was to drive me from his country home into the town of Lowry, Minnesota, in time for me to take an afternoon train for Winnipeg, on which I had a Pullman reservation. I can remember yet how I urged my friend to get on the way, but he puttered about with all kinds of inconsequential chores, insistent that there was plenty of time. I fumed and fretted to no purpose. He was calmly adamant.

Finally, he hitched up his team and we started across the prairie. About a mile from town we saw the train steam into the station, pause a few moments, and depart for the north. There was nothing to do but wait some five or six hours for the night express, on which I had no reservation, and found when it arrived

I could not get a berth, so was obliged to sit in a crowded day coach all the way to the Canadian border, after which there was more room. While annoyed, I comforted myself with the words, "And we know that all things work together for good to them that love God, to them who are the called according to his purpose." I prayed earnestly that if He had some purpose in permitting me to miss my train and comfortable accommodations, I might not fail to find it out.

When I boarded the crowded, foul-smelling coach, I found there was only one vacancy left and that was half of a seat midway down the car, a sleeping young man occupying the other half. As I sat down by him and stowed away my baggage, he awoke, straightened up, and gave me a rather sleepy greeting. Soon we were in an agreeable, low-toned conversation, while other passengers slept and snored all about us. A suitable opportunity presenting itself, I inquired, "Do you know the Lord Jesus Christ?" He sat up as though shot. "How strange that you should ask me that! I went to sleep thinking of Him and wishing I did know Him, but I do not understand, though I want to! Can you help me?"

Further conversation elicited the fact that he had been working in a town in southern Minnesota, where he had been persuaded to attend some revival meetings. Evidently, the preaching was in power and he became deeply concerned about his soul. He had even gone forward to the mourners' bench, but though he wept and prayed over his sins, he came away without finding peace. I knew then why I had missed my train. This was my Gaza, and though unworthy I was sent

of God to be His Philip. So I opened to the same
scripture that the Ethiopian treasurer had been reading
when Philip met him—Isaiah 53.

Drawing my newly found friend's attention to its
wonderful depiction of the crucified Saviour, though
written so long before the event, I put before him
verses 4, 5 and 6: "Surely he hath borne our griefs,
and carried our sorrows: yet we did esteem him
stricken, smitten of God, and afflicted. But he was
wounded for our transgressions, he was bruised for
our iniquities: the chastisement of our peace was upon
him; and with his stripes we are healed. All we like
sheep have gone astray; we have turned every one to
his own way; and the LORD hath laid on him the
iniquity of us all."

As the young man read them, they seemed to burn
their way into his very soul. He saw himself as the lost
sheep that had taken its own way. He saw Christ as
the One on whom Jehovah laid all his iniquity, and
he bowed his head and told Him he would trust Him
as his own Saviour. For perhaps two hours we had
hallowed fellowship on the way, as we turned from one
scripture to another. Then he reached his destination
and left, thanking me most profusely for showing him
the way of life. I have never seen him since, but I
know I shall greet him again at the judgment seat of
Christ.

Help for the Needy Soul

Into whose hands this book will fall I cannot tell,
but I send it forth with the prayer that it may prove

as timely a message to many a needy soul as the talk on the train that night in Minnesota with the young man who felt his need and had really turned to God, but did not understand the way of peace and so had no assurance, until he found it through the written Word, borne home to his soul in the power of the Holy Spirit.

If you are just as troubled as that young man, and should by divine providence use this treatise at any time, I trust that you will see that it is the Lord's own way of seeking to draw you to Himself, and that you will read it carefully, thoughtfully, and prayerfully, looking up each passage referred to in your own Bible, if you have one, and that thus you, too, may obtain full assurance.

Be certain of this: God is deeply concerned about you. He longs to give you the knowledge of His salvation. It is no mere accident that these pages have come to your attention. He put it on my heart to write them. He would have you read them. They may prove to be His own message to your troubled soul. God's ways are varied. "He worketh all things after the counsel of his own will."

The Barber Was Much Concerned

Another personal experience will perhaps accentuate and fittingly close this chapter. One afternoon I was walking the busy streets of Indianapolis, looking for a barber shop. Entering the first one I saw (my attention being attracted by the red and white striped pole), I was soon seated in the chair, and the tonsorial artist began operations. He was chatty but subdued, I thought,

not carelessly voluble. Praying for an opening, it soon
seemed a fitting time to ask as in the other case, "Are
you acquainted with the Lord Jesus Christ?" To my
astonishment, the barber's reaction was remarkable. He
stopped his work, burst into uncontrollable weeping,
and when the first paroxysm had passed, exclaimed,
"How strange that you should ask me about Him! In
all my life I never had a man ask me that before. And
I have been thinking of Him nearly all the time for
the last three days. What can you tell me about Him?"

It was my turn to be amazed. I asked him what had
led up to this. He explained that he had gone to see
a picture of a passion play, and that it had made an
indelible impression on his mind. He kept asking,
"Why did that good Man have to suffer so? Why
did God let Him die like that?" He had never
heard the gospel in his life, so I spent an hour with
him opening up the story of the cross. We prayed
together and he declared that all was now plain, and
he trusted the Saviour for himself. I had the joy of
knowing, as I left his shop, that the gospel was indeed
the dynamic of God unto salvation to him, an uninstructed Greek barber, who had learned for the first
time that Christ loved him and gave Himself for him.

To me it was a singular instance of divine sover-
eignty. The very idea of a passion play—sinful men
endeavoring to portray the life, death and resurrection
of Jesus—was abhorrent to me. But God, who delights
not in the death of the sinner, but desires that all
should turn to Him and live, used that very picture
to arouse this man and so make him ready to hear the
gospel. And I could not doubt that He had directed my

steps to that particular shop, that I might have the joy of pointing the anxious barber to the Lamb of God that taketh away the sin of the world.

That in many similar instances He may be pleased to own and use these written messages is my earnest desire.

> Sovereign grace o'er sin abounding,
>   Ransomed souls the tidings tell;
> 'Tis a deep that knows no sounding,
>   Who its length and breadth can tell?
> On its glories, let my soul forever dwell.

2

ASSURANCE FOREVER

THERE IS a very remarkable statement found in Isaiah 32:17: "The work of righteousness shall be peace; and the effect of righteousness quietness and assurance forever."

Assurance forever! Is it not a wonderfully pleasing expression? Assurance not for a few days, or weeks, or months—nor yet for a few years, or even a lifetime—but forever! It is this blessed assurance that God delights to impart to all who come to Him as needy sinners seeking the way of life.

Two words are employed in this verse that are intimately related—peace and assurance. Yet how many deeply religious people there are in the world who scarcely know the meaning of either term. They are honestly seeking after God. They are punctilious about their religious duties, such as reading the Scriptures, saying their prayers, attending church, partaking of the sacrament, and supporting the cause of Christ. They are scrupulously honest and upright in all their dealings with their fellowmen, endeavoring to fulfill every civic and national responsibility, and to obey the golden rule. Yet they have no lasting peace, nor any definite assurance of salvation. I am persuaded that in practically every such instance the reason for their unquiet and unsettled state is due to a lack of apprehension of God's way of salvation.

Though living seven centuries before Calvary, it was given to Isaiah to set forth in a very blessed manner the righteousness of God as later revealed in the gospel. This is not to be wondered at for he spoke as he was moved by the Holy Spirit.

The key word of his great book, often called the fifth gospel, is the same as in the epistle to the Romans —the word, "righteousness." And I would urge the reader to meditate on this word for a little and see how it is used in the Holy Scriptures.

The Dying Lawyer

A lawyer lay dying. He had attended church all his life but was not saved. He was known to be a man of unimpeachable integrity. Yet as he lay there facing eternity, he was troubled and distressed. He knew that upright as he had been before men, he was a sinner before God. His awakened conscience brought to his memory sins and transgressions that had never seemed so heinous as then, when he knew that shortly he must meet his Maker.

A friend put the direct question, "Are you saved?" He replied in the negative, shaking his head sadly. The other asked, "Would you not like to be saved?" "I would indeed," was his reply, "if it is not already too late. But," he added almost fiercely, "I do not want God to do anything wrong in saving me!"

His remark showed how deeply he had learned to value the importance of righteousness. The visitor turned to his Bible and there read how God had

Himself devised a righteous way to save unrighteous sinners. The fact is that He has no other possible way of saving anybody. If sin must be glossed over, in order that the sinner may be saved, he will be forever lost. God refuses to compromise His own character for the sake of anyone, much as He yearns to have all men to be saved.

It was this that stirred the soul of Luther, and brought new light and help after long, weary months of groping in the darkness, trying in vain to save himself in conformity to the demands of blind leaders of the blind. As he was reading the Latin Psalter, he came across David's prayer, "Save me in thy righteousness." Luther exclaimed, "What does this mean? I can understand how God can damn me in His righteousness, but if He would save me it must surely be in His mercy!" The more he meditated on it, the more the wonder grew. But little by little the truth dawned upon his troubled soul that God Himself had devised a righteous method whereby He could justify unrighteous sinners who came to Him in repentance and received His Word in faith.

Isaiah stresses this great and glorious truth throughout his marvelous Old Testament unfolding of the gospel plan. In unsparing severity, the prophet portrays man's utterly lost and absolutely hopeless condition, apart from divine grace. "The whole head is sick, and the whole heart faint. From the sole of the foot even unto the head there is no soundness in it; but wounds and bruises and putrefying sores: they have not been closed, neither bound up, neither mollified with ointment" (Isa. 1:5-6). It is surely a revolting picture, but nevertheless it is true of the unsaved man as God sees him. Sin is a vile disease that has fastened upon the very vitals of its victim. None can free himself from its pollution, or deliver himself from its power.

A Sure Remedy

But God has a remedy. He says, "Come now, and let us reason together, saith the LORD: though your sins be as scarlet, they shall be as white as snow; though they be red like crimson, they shall be as wool" (v. 18). It is God Himself who can thus purge the leper from all his uncleanness, and justify the ungodly from all his guilt. And He does it, not at the expense of righteousness, but in a perfectly righteous way.

> 'Tis in the Cross of Christ we see
> How God can save, yet righteous be;
> 'Tis in the Cross of Christ we trace
> His righteousness and wondrous grace.
> The sinner who believes is free,
> Can say, the Saviour died for me;
> Can point to the atoning blood
> And say, that made my peace with God.

So it is Isaiah who, above all other prophetic writers, sets forth the work of the cross. He looks on by the eye of faith to Calvary, and there he sees the holy Sufferer dying for sins not His own. He exclaims, "He was wounded for our transgressions, he was bruised for our iniquities: the chastisement of our peace was upon him; and with his stripes we are healed. All we like sheep have gone astray; we have turned every one to his own way; and the LORD [Jehovah] hath laid on him the iniquity of us all" (Isa. 53:5-6).

Have you ever thoughtfully considered these remarkable statements? If not, I beg you to ponder over them now. It was Jesus that the Spirit of God brought before the mind of Isaiah. He would have you gaze upon Him, too. Take each clause separately and weigh its wondrous meaning.

"He was wounded for our transgressions." Make it personal! Put yourself and your own sins in there. Read it as though it said, "He was wounded for *my* transgressions." Do not get lost in the crowd. If there had never been another sinner in the world, Jesus would have gone to the cross for you! Oh, believe it and enter into peace!

"He was bruised for our iniquities." Make it personal! Think what your ungodliness and your self-will cost Him. He took the blows that should have fallen upon you. He stepped in between you and God, as the rod of justice was about to fall. It bruised Him in your stead. Again, I plead, make it personal! Cry out in faith, "He was bruised for my iniquities."

Now go further. "The chastisement of our peace was upon him." All that was necessary to make peace with God, He endured. "He made peace through the blood of his cross." Change the "our" to "my." "He made *my* peace."

> He bore on the tree
> The sentence for me,
> And now both the surety
> And sinner are free.

Now note the last clause of this glorious verse, "With his stripes we are healed." Do you see it? Can you set

to your seal that God is true, and cry exultingly, "Yes,
I a poor sinner, I a lost, ruined soul, I who so richly
deserved judgment, I am healed by His stripes"?

> We are healed by His stripes,
>   Wouldst thou add to the Word?
> He Himself is our righteousness made.
>   The best robe of heaven He bids thee put on,
> Oh, couldst thou be better arrayed?

The Old Account Settled

It is not that God ignores our sins, or indulgently
overlooks them; but on the cross all have been settled
for. In Isaiah 53:6, He has balanced the books of the
world. There were two debit entries:

> All we like sheep have gone astray;
> We have turned every one to his own way.

But there is one credit item that squares the account:

> Jehovah hath laid on him [that is, on Jesus at
> the cross] the iniquity of us all.

The first debit entry takes into account our partici-
pation in the fall of the race. Sheep follow the leader.
One goes through a hole in the fence and all follow
after. So Adam sinned and we are all implicated in his
guilt. "Death passed upon all men, for that all have
sinned."

But the second entry takes into account our individual willfulness. Each one has chosen to sin in his
own way, so we are not only sinners by nature, but
we are also transgressors by practice. In other words,
we are lost—utterly lost. But "the Son of man is come
to seek and to save that which was lost" (Luke 19:10).

By His sacrificial death on the cross, He has paid to outraged justice that which meets every charge against the sinner. Now in perfect righteousness God can offer a complete pardon and justification to all who trust His risen Son.

Thus "the work of righteousness shall be peace; and the effect of righteousness quietness and assurance forever." The troubled conscience can now be at rest. God is satisfied with what His Son has done. On that basis He can freely forgive the vilest sinner who turns in repentance to the Christ of the cross.

> The trembling sinner feareth
>   That God can ne'er forget;
> But one full payment cleareth
>   His mem'ry of all debt;
> Returning sons He kisses,
>   And with His robe invests;
> His perfect love dismisses
>   All terror from our breasts.

He says to every believing soul, "I have blotted out, as a thick cloud, thy transgressions, and, as a cloud, thy sins: return unto me; for I have redeemed thee" (Isa. 44:22). And again, "I, even I, am he that blotteth out thy transgressions for mine own sake, and will not remember thy sins" (Isa. 43:25). You may never be able to forget the years of wandering, the many sins of which you have been guilty. But that which gives peace is the knowledge that God will never recall them again. He has blotted them from the book of His remembrance, and He has done it in righteousness, for the account is completely settled. The debt is paid!

Christ's Resurrection Gives Assurance

Christ's bodily resurrection is the divine token that all has been dealt with to God's satisfaction. Jesus bore our sins on the cross. He made Himself responsible for them. He died to put them away forever. But God raised Him from the dead, thereby attesting His good pleasure in the work of His Son. Now the blessed Lord sits exalted at the right hand of the Majesty in the heavens. He could not be there if our sins were still upon Him. The fact that He is there proves that they are completely put away. God is satisfied!

> Payment He will not twice demand,
> First at my bleeding Surety's hand,
> And then again at mine.

It is this that gives quietness and assurance forever. When I know that my sins have been dealt with in such a way that God's righteousness remains untarnished, even as He folds me to His bosom, a justified believer, I have perfect peace. I know Him now as "a just God and a Saviour" (Isa. 45:21). He says, "I will bring near my righteousness; it shall not be far off, and my salvation shall not tarry" (Isa. 46:13). What cheering words are these! He has provided a righteousness, *His very own,* for men who have *none of their own!* Gladly, therefore, do I spurn all attempts at self-righteousness, to be found in Him perfect and complete, clothed with His righteousness.

Every believer can say with the prophet, "I will greatly rejoice in the LORD, my soul shall be joyful in my God; for he hath clothed me with the garments of salvation, he hath covered me with the robe of righteousness, as a bridegroom decketh himself with ornaments, and as a bride adorneth herself with jewels" (Isa. 61:10).

> Clad in this robe, how bright I shine;
> Angels have not a robe like mine.

It is given only to redeemed sinners to wear this garment of glory. Christ Himself *is* the robe of righteousness. We who trust him are "in Christ"; we are "made the righteousness of God in him" (II Cor. 5:21). He is "made unto us wisdom, and righteousness, and sanctification, and redemption" (I Cor. 1:30). If my acceptance depended on my growth in grace I could never have settled peace. It would be egotism of the worst kind to consider myself so holy that I could be satisfactory to God on the ground of my personal experience. But when I see that "he hath made us accepted in the beloved," every doubt is banished. My soul is at peace. I have quietness and assurance forever. I know now that only

> That which can shake the Cross,
>   Can shake the peace it gave;
> Which tells me Christ has never died,
>   Nor ever left the grave.

As long as these great unchanging verities remain, my peace is unshaken, my confidence is secure. I have "assurance forever."

Dear, anxious, burdened soul, do you not see it? Can you not rest, where God rests, in the finished work of His blessed Son? If He is satisfied to save you by faith in Jesus, surely you should be satisfied to trust Him.

3

MUCH ASSURANCE

W HEN REMINDING the Thessalonian believers of the work of God in their city, as a result of which they were saved, the Apostle Paul says: "We give thanks to God always for you all, making mention of you in our prayers; remembering without ceasing your work of faith, and labor of love, and patience of hope in our Lord Jesus Christ, in the sight of God and our Father; knowing, brethren beloved, your election of God. For our gospel came not unto you in word only, but also in power, and in the Holy Ghost, and in much assurance; as ye know what manner of men we were among you for your sake. And ye became followers of us, and of the Lord, having received the word in much affliction, with joy of the Holy Ghost: so that ye were ensamples to all that believe in Macedonia and Achaia."

This is a very striking declaration, and all the more so because it stands out in such vivid contrast with much that goes under the name of evangelical testimony in our days. It is not too much to say of perhaps the majority of sermons preached in our myriads of churches, that one who was in deep spiritual trouble might listen to them year in and year out and be left in as great uncertainty as ever. They give no assurance

to the hearers, whereas Paul's preaching was of such
a character as to produce *much* assurance.

Consider the people addressed. Only a few months
before at the most, they were for the greater part
pagan idolaters, living in all kinds of sin and uncleanness. They had never been trained in Christian truth.
A few among them were Jews, and had some knowledge of the law and the prophets. But the great majority by far were ignorant heathen, given to superstitious
and licentious practices, and who were without any
understanding of the way of life.

To them came Paul and his little company of
itinerant preachers—men of God whose lives evidenced
the power of the message they proclaimed. In dependence on the Holy Spirit they preached Jesus Christ
and Him crucified. They bore witness to His resurrection and present saving power, and they declared He
was coming back some day to be Judge of the living
and the dead. It was the same missionary message
which has ever proven to be the dynamic of God unto
salvation to all who believe. Paul's hearers were convicted of their sin. They realized something of the
corruption of their lives. They turned to God as
repentant sinners, and believed the gospel they heard
preached. What was the result? They became new
creatures. Their outward behavior reflected the inward
change. They knew they had passed out of darkness
into light. They did not simply cherish a pious hope
that God had received them. They knew He had made
them His own. They had much assurance! Could anything be more blessed?

Is it not strange that so much that passes for gospel

preaching today fails to produce this very-much-to-be-desired result? Surely something is radically wrong when people can be churchgoers all their lives and never get further than to live in hope of receiving "dying grace" at last!

The Woman Was Dying

An aged woman was reported to be dying. Her physician had given up all hope of her recovery. Her minister was called to her bedside to prepare her for the great change. She was in much distress. Bitterly she lamented her sins, her coldness of heart, her feeble efforts to serve the Lord. Piteously, she besought her pastor to give what help he could that dying grace might indeed be hers. The good man was plainly disconcerted. He was not used to coming to close quarters with dying souls anxious to be sure of salvation. But he quoted and read various scriptures. His eye fell on the words, "Not by works of righteousness which we have done, but according to his mercy he saved us, by the washing of regeneration, and renewing of the Holy Ghost; which he shed on us abundantly through Jesus Christ our Saviour; that being justified by his grace, we should be made heirs according to the hope of eternal life" (Titus 3:5-7).

As he read the words with quivering voice, the dying woman drank in their truth. "Not by works, but justified by His grace!" she exclaimed. "Aye, minister, that'll do; I can rest there. No works of mine to plead, just to trust His grace. That will do. I can die in peace." He prayed with her and left, his own heart tenderly moved and grateful, too, that he had been used to minister dying grace to this troubled member of his flock. He hardly expected to see her again on earth, but was comforted to feel that she would soon be in heaven.

Contrary to her physician's prediction, however, she did not die but rallied from that very hour, and in a few weeks was well again, a happy, rejoicing believer with much assurance. She sent once more for the pastor, and put the strange question to him, "God has given me dying grace and now I am well again; what am I to do about it?"

"Ah, woman," he exclaimed, "ye may just claim it as living grace and abide in the joy of it."

It was well put, but what a pity his preaching throughout the years had not produced assurance long before in the mind and heart of his anxious parishioner.

The Thessalonian believers did not have to wait until facing death in order to enter into the positive knowledge of sins forgiven. Their election of God was a reality to themselves and to others, who saw what grace had wrought in their lives.

And it was what Paul calls "our gospel," and "my gospel," that produced all this. We are not left in any doubt as to what that gospel was, for he has made it very clear elsewhere. He had but one message, that Christ died for our sins, was buried, and rose again. The import of this received in faith destroyed doubt, banished uncertainty, and produced much assurance.

Of course, back of the witness borne by the lips was the witness of the life. Paul's deportment among them was that of a man who lived in the atmosphere of eternity. A holy minister of Christ preaching a clear gospel in the energy of the Holy Spirit is bound to get results. Such a man is a tremendous weapon in the hand of God for the pulling down of satanic strongholds. But it was not the piety of the messengers that gave assurance to those early believers. It was the message itself which they received in faith.

It is a great mistake to attempt to rest one's soul upon the character of any preacher, however godly he may appear to be. Faith is to rest, not in the best of God's servants but in His unchanging Word. Unhappily, it often transpires that impressionable folk are carried away with admiration for a minister of Christ, and they put their dependence upon him, rather than upon the truth proclaimed.

"I was converted by Billy Sunday himself!" said one to me, in answer to the question, "Are you certain that your soul is saved?"

Mr. Sunday would have been the last of men to put himself in the place of Christ. Further conversation seemed to elicit the evidence that the person in question had been carried away by admiration for the earnest evangelist and mistook the "thrill of a handshake" for the Spirit's witness. At least, there seemed no real understanding of God's plan of salvation, which Billy Sunday preached in such tremendous power.

Then it is well to remember that some vivid emotional experience is not a safe ground of assurance. It is the blood of Christ that makes us safe and the Word of God that makes us sure.

Queen Victoria Decides the Question

There is an apparently authentic story told of the great Queen Victoria, so long ruler of Britain's vast empire. When she occupied her castle at Balmoral, Scotland, she was in the habit of calling, in a friendly way, upon certain cottagers living in the neighborhood. One aged highland woman, who felt greatly honored by these visits and who knew the Lord, was anxious about the soul of the queen. As the season came to a close one year, her Majesty was making her last visit to the humble home of this dear child of God. After the good-byes were said, the old cottager timidly inquired, "May I ask your gracious Majesty a question?"

"Yes," replied the queen, "as many as you like."

"Will your Majesty meet me in heaven?"

Instantly the royal visitor replied, "I will, through the all-availing blood of Jesus."

That is the only safe ground for assurance. The blood shed on Calvary avails for all classes alike.

When Israel of old was about to leave Egypt, and the last awful plague was to fall on that land and its people, God Himself provided a way of escape for His own. They were to slay a lamb, sprinkle its blood on the doorposts and lintel of their houses, go inside and shut the door. When the destroying angel passed through that night, he would not be permitted to enter any blood-sprinkled door, for Jehovah had said, "When I see the blood, I will pass over you." Inside the house, some might have been trembling and some rejoicing, but *all* were safe. Their security depended, not on their frames of mind, or feelings, but on the fact that the eye of God beheld the blood of the lamb and they

were sheltered behind it. As they recalled the word
that He had given concerning it and truly believed it,
they would have much assurance.

So it is today! We cannot see the blood shed so
long ago for our redemption on Calvary, but there
is a sense in which it is ever before the eye of God.
The moment a repentant sinner puts his trust in Christ,
he is viewed by God as sheltered behind the blood-
sprinkled lintel. Henceforth his security from judgment depends, not on his ability to satisfy the righteous
demands of the holy One, but upon the blessed fact
that Christ Jesus satisfied them to the utmost when He
gave Himself a ransom for our sins, and thus made it
possible for God to pass over all our offences and
justify us from all things.

That Dreadful Night in Egypt

Imagine a Jewish youth on that night in Egypt reasoning thus: "I am the firstborn of this family and in
thousands of homes tonight the firstborn must die. I
wish I could be sure that I was safe and secure, but
when I think of my many shortcomings, I am in deep-
est distress and perplexity. I do not feel that I am by
any means good enough to be saved when others must
die. I have been very willful, very disobedient, very
undependable, and now I feel so troubled and anxious.
I question very much if I shall see the morning light."

Would his anxiety and self-condemnation leave him
exposed to judgment? Surely not! His father might
well say to him, "Son, what you say as to yourself is
all true. Not one of us has ever been all he should be.
We all deserve to die. But the death of the lamb was

for you—the lamb died in your stead. The blood of
the lamb outside the house comes between you and
the destroyer."

One can understand how the young man's face
would light up as he exclaimed, "Ah, I see it! It is
not what I am that saves me from judgment. It is the
blood and I am safe behind the blood-sprinkled door."
Thus he would have much assurance. And in the same
way, we now, who trust in the testimony God has given
concerning the atoning work of His Son, enter into
peace and know we are free from all condemnation.

Perhaps someone may ask, "But does it make no
difference to God what I am myself? May I live on in
my sins and still be saved?" No, assuredly not! But
this brings in another line of truth. The moment one
believes the gospel, he is born again and receives a
new life and nature—a nature that hates sin and loves
holiness. If you have come to Jesus and trusted Him,
do you not realize the truth of this? Do you not now
hate and detest the wicked things that once gave you
a certain degree of delight? Do you not find within
yourself a new craving for goodness, a longing after
holiness, and a thirst for righteousness? All this is the
evidence of a new nature. And as you walk with God
you will find that daily the power of the indwelling
Holy Spirit will give you practical deliverance from
the dominion of sin.

This line of truth does not touch the question of
your salvation. It is the outcome of your salvation.
First, get this settled. You are justified not by anything
done in you, but by what Jesus did for you on the
cross. But now He who died for you works in you to

conform you daily to Himself, and to enable you to manifest in a devoted life the reality of His salvation.

The Thessalonians "turned to God from idols to serve the living and true God; and to wait for his Son from heaven." The moment they turned to Him they were saved, forgiven, justified, set apart to God in all the value of the work of the cross and the perfection of the resurrected life of the Lord Jesus. They were accepted in the Beloved! God saw them in Christ. Believing thus, they had much assurance.

This matter settled, they then yielded themselves unto God as those alive from the dead, to serve Him who had done so much for them, and they waited day by day for the coming again of Him who had died for them, whom God had raised from the dead and seated at His right hand in highest glory.

Acceptable service springs from the knowledge that the question of salvation is forever settled. We who are saved by grace apart from all self-effort are "created in Christ Jesus unto good works, which God hath before ordained that we should walk in them."

Not Saved by Good Works

Notice, we are not saved *by* good works, but *unto* good works. In other words, no one can begin to live a Christian life until he has a Christian life to live. This life is divine and eternal. It is imparted by God Himself to the one who believes the gospel, as the Apostle Peter tells us: "Being born again, not of corruptible seed, but of incorruptible, by the word of God, which liveth and abideth forever. For all flesh is as

grass, and all the glory of man as the flower of grass.
The grass withereth, and the flower thereof falleth away:
but the word of the Lord endureth forever. And this
is the word which by the gospel is preached unto you"
(I Peter 1:23-25).

The new birth, therefore, is by the Word—the message of the gospel—and the power of the Holy Spirit.
"That which is born of the flesh is flesh; and that
which is born of the Spirit is spirit." These were our
Lord's words to Nicodemus. The one thus regenerated
has eternal life and can never perish. How do we
know? Because He has told us so.

Weigh carefully the precious words of John 5:24,
"Verily, verily, I say unto you, He that heareth my
word, and believeth on him that sent me, hath everlasting life, and shall not come into condemnation;
but is passed from death unto life"; and link with this
verse John 10:27-30, "My sheep hear my voice, and
I know them, and they follow me: and I give unto
them eternal life; and they shall never perish, neither
shall any man pluck them out of my hand. My Father,
which gave them me, is greater than all; and no man
is able to pluck them out of my Father's hand. I and
my Father are one."

Observe that in the first of these passages there are
five links, all of which go together: "Heareth . . .
believeth . . . hath . . . shall not . . . is passed." Study
these terms carefully and note their true connection.
They should never be dissociated. In the longer passage pay careful attention to what is said of Christ's
sheep:

    a. They hear His voice.
    b. They follow Him.
    c. They possess eternal life.
    d. They shall never perish.
    e. None can pluck them from the hands of
        the Father and the Son.

Could there be greater security than this and could any words give clearer assurance of the complete salvation of all who come to God through His Son? To doubt His testimony is to make God a liar. To believe His record is to have much assurance.

Do you say, "I will try to believe"? Try to believe whom? Dare you speak in this way of the living God who will never call back His words? If an earthly friend told you a remarkable tale that seemed hard to credit, would you say, "I will try to believe you"? To do so would be to insult him to his face. And will you so treat the God of truth, whose gifts and promises are never revoked? Rather look up to Him, confessing all the unbelief of the past as sin, trust Him now, and thus know that you are one of the redeemed.

Some years ago in St. Louis, a worker was dealing with a man who had expressed his desire to be saved by going into the inquiry room upon the invitation of the evangelist. The worker endeavored to show the man that the way to be saved was by accepting Christ as his Saviour and believing the promise of God. But the man kept saying: "I can't believe; I can't believe!"

"Who can't you believe?" replied the worker.

"Who can't I believe?" said the man.

"Yes, who can't you believe? Can't you believe God? He cannot lie."

"Why, yes," said the man, "I can believe God; but I had never thought of it in that way before. I thought you had to have some sort of feeling."

The man had been trying to work up a sense of faith, instead of relying upon the sure promise of God. For the first time he realized that he was to take God at His word, and as he did so, he experienced the power and assurance of salvation.

> Not saved are we by trying;
>   From self can come no aid;
> 'Tis on the blood relying,
>   Once for our ransom paid.
> 'Tis looking unto Jesus,
>   The Holy One and Just;
> 'Tis His great work that saves us—
>   It is not "try" but "trust"!
>
> No deeds of ours are needed
>   To make Christ's merit more:
> No frames of mind or feelings
>   Can add to His great store;
> 'Tis simply to receive Him,
>   The Holy One and Just;
> 'Tis only to believe Him—
>   It is not "try" but "trust"!

4

FULL ASSURANCE OF FAITH

IN THE TENTH CHAPTER of the epistle to the Hebrews, verses 19-22, are found the words which we will consider together as the theme of this present chapter. Read the entire passage very thoughtfully: "Having therefore, brethren, boldness to enter into the holiest by the blood of Jesus, by a new and living way, which he hath consecrated for us, through the veil, that is to say, his flesh; and having an high priest over the house of God; let us draw near with a true heart in full assurance of faith, having our hearts sprinkled from an evil conscience, and our bodies washed with pure water" (Heb. 10:19-22).

Do you notice that remarkable expression "full assurance of faith"? Does it not thrill your soul as you read it? "Full assurance!" What could be more precious? And it is for you if you want it, only you must receive it by faith. For observe carefully, it is not the full assurance of an emotional experience, nor the full assurance of a carefully reasoned-out system of philosophy. It is the full assurance of faith.

The little boy was right who replied to his teacher's question, "What is faith?" by exclaiming, "Faith is believing God and asking no questions." That is exactly what it is. Faith is taking God at His word. This is the real meaning of that wonderful definition given by inspiration in Hebrews 11:1, "Now faith is the substance of things hoped for, the evidence of things not seen." God tells us something beyond human understanding. Faith gives substance to that. It makes unseen things even more real than things that the eye beholds. It relies in unquestioning certainty upon what God has declared to be true. And when there is this complete reliance upon the promise of God, the Holy Spirit bears witness to the truth, so that the believer has the full assurance of faith.

Faith is not, however, mere intellectual acceptance of certain facts. It involves trust and confidence in those facts, and this results in the word of faith and the work of faith. Faith in Christ is not, therefore, simply accrediting the historical statements revealed concerning our blessed Lord. It is to trust oneself wholly to Him in reliance upon His redemptive work. To believe is to trust. To trust is to have faith. To have faith in Christ is to have full assurance of salvation.

Because this is so, faith must have something tangible to lay hold of, some definite worthwhile message to rest upon. And it is just this that is set forth in the gospel, which is God's well-ordered plan of salvation for sinners who otherwise are lost, helpless and hopeless.

When, for instance, we are told four times in our Bibles that "the just shall live by faith," it is not simply that we live in a spirit of optimism, a faith or hope that everything will come out all right at last. And when we speak of the doctrine of justification by faith, it is not to say that he who maintains a courageous heart will thereby be declared righteous. Faith is not the savior. Faith is the hand that lays hold of Him who does save. Therefore the folly of talking of weak faith as opposed to strong faith. The feeblest faith in Christ is saving faith. The strongest faith in self, or something other than Christ, is but a delusion and a snare, and will leave the soul at last unsaved and forever forlorn.

And so when we are bidden to draw near to God with true hearts in full assurance of faith, the meaning is that we are to rest implicitly on what God has revealed concerning His Son and His glorious work for our redemption. This is set forth admirably in the former part of this chapter in Hebrews where our verse is found. There we have set out in vivid contrast the difference between the many sacrifices offered under the legal dispensation and the one perfect, all-sufficient oblation of our Lord Jesus Christ. Note some of the outstanding differences:

1. They were many and often repeated. His is but one, and no other will ever be required.

2. They did not have the necessary value to settle the sin question. His is of such infinite value, it has settled that problem forevermore.

3. They could not purge the consciences of those who brought them. His purges all who believe, giving a perfect conscience because all sin has been put away from under the eye of God.

4. They could not open the way into the holiest. His has rent the veil, and inaugurated the new and living way into the very presence of God.

5. They could not perfect the one who offered them. His one sacrifice has perfected forever those who are sanctified.

6. In them there was a remembrance again of sins from year to year. His has enabled God to say, "Their sins and iniquities will I remember no more."

7. It was not possible that the blood of bulls and of goats should put away sin. But Christ has accomplished that very thing by the sacrifice of Himself.

Here then is where faith rests, on the finished work of Christ. It will help us greatly to understand this, if we glance at what is revealed concerning the sin offering of the old dispensation.

Consider the Troubled Israelite

Let us imagine that we stand near the altar in the temple court, as a troubled Israelite comes with his sacrifice. He leads a goat along to the place of the oblation. The priest examines it carefully, and finding it without any outward blemish he commands it to be slain. The offerer himself puts the knife to its throat, after laying his hand on its head. Then it is flayed and cut in pieces, and all its inward parts carefully inspected. Pronounced perfect, it is accepted and certain parts are placed upon the fire of the altar. The blood is sprinkled round about the altar and upon its four horns, after which the priest pronounces absolution, assuring the man of his forgiveness.

This was but "a shadow of good things to come," and could not actually put away sin. That unblemished animal typified the sinless Saviour who became the great sin offering. His blood has made full and complete expiation for iniquity. All who come to God through Him are eternally forgiven.

If the Israelite sinned against the Lord, on the morrow he required a new sacrifice. His conscience was never made perfect. But Christ's one offering is of such infinite value that it settles the sin question eternally for all who put their trust in Him. "By one offering he hath perfected forever them that are sanctified." To be sanctified in this sense is to be set apart to God in all the value of the atoning work and the personal perfections of Christ. He is Himself our sanctification. God sees us henceforth in His Son.

Is not this a wonderfully precious truth? It is something man would never have dreamed of. God alone devised such a plan. He who believes His testimony regarding it has full assurance of faith.

He does not know he is saved because he feels happy. But every true believer will be happy to know he is saved.

Confidence based upon an emotional experience would leave one in utter bewilderment when that emotion passed away. But assurance based upon the Word of God abides, because that Word is unchangeable.

The Old Gentleman Had No Peace

Many years ago I was holding a series of evangelistic meetings in a little country schoolhouse some miles out of Santa Cruz, California. One day I was out driving with a kindly old gentleman who was attending the services nightly, but who was far from being sure of his personal salvation. As we drove along a beautiful, winding road, literally embowered with great trees, I put the definite question to him, "Have you peace with God?" He drew rein at once, stopped the horse, and exclaimed, "Now that's what I brought you here for. I won't go another foot until I know I am saved, or else know it is hopeless to seek to be sure of it."

"How do you expect to find out?" I inquired.

"Well, that is what puzzles me. I want a definite witness, something that I cannot be mistaken about."

"Just what would you consider definite, some inward emotional stirring?"

"I can hardly say, only most folks tell us they felt some powerful change when they got religion. I have been seeking that for years, but it has always eluded me."

"Getting religion is one thing; trusting Christ may be quite another. But now suppose you were seeking salvation, and suddenly there came to you a very happy feeling, would you be sure then that you were saved?"

"Well, I think I would."

"Then, suppose you went through life resting on that experience, and at last came down to the hour of death. Imagine Satan telling you that you were lost and would soon be beyond hope of mercy, what would you say to him? Would you tell him that you knew all was well, because you had such a happy emotional experience years before? What if he should declare that it was he who gave you that happy feeling, in order to deceive you, could you prove it was not?"

"No," he answered thoughtfully, "I couldn't. I see that a happy feeling is not enough."

"What would be enough?"

"If I could get some definite word in a vision, or a message from an angel, then I could be sure."

"But suppose you had a vision of a glorious angel, and he told you your sins were forgiven, would that really be enough to rest on?"

"I think it would. One ought to be certain if an angel said it was all right."

"But if you were dying and Satan was there to disturb you, and told you that you were lost after all, what could you say?"

"Why, I'd tell him an angel told me I was saved."

"But if he said, 'I was that angel. I transformed myself into an angel of light to deceive you. And now you are where I wanted you—you will be lost forever.' What then could you say?"

He pondered a moment or two, and then replied, "I see, you are right; the word of an angel won't do."

"But now," I said, "God has given something better than happy feelings, something more dependable than the voice of an angel. He has given His Son to die for your sins, and He has testified in His own unalterable Word that if you trust in Him all your sins are gone. Listen to this: 'To him give all the prophets witness, that through his name whosoever believeth in him shall receive remission of sins.' These are the words of God spoken through His apostle Peter, as recorded in Acts 10:43.

"Then here is I John 5:13, which says, 'These things have I written unto you that believe on the name of the Son of God; that ye may know that ye have eternal life.' Are these words addressed to you? Do you believe on the name of the Son of God?"

"I do, sir, I do indeed! I know He is the Son of God, and I know He died for me."

"Then see what He tells you, 'Ye may *know* that ye *have* eternal life.' Is not this enough to rest upon? It is a letter from heaven directed expressly to you. How can you refuse to accept what God has told you? Can you not believe Him? Is He not more to be depended on than an angel, or than aroused emotions? Can you not take Him at His word and rest upon it for the forgiveness of your sins?

"Now suppose that as you are dying Satan comes to you and insists that you are lost, but you reply, 'No, Satan, you cannot terrify me now. I rest on the Word of the living God and He tells me I *have* eternal life, and also the remission of all my sins.' Can you not do this now? Will you not bow your head and tell God you will be saved on His terms by coming to Him as a repentant sinner and trusting His Word concerning His blessed Son?"

The old man dropped his eyes, and I saw that he was deeply stirred. His lips were moving in prayer. Suddenly he looked up and touching the horse lightly with his whip, exclaimed, "Giddap! It's all clear now. This is what I've wanted for years."

That night at the meeting he came to the front and told the audience that what he had sought in vain for half a lifetime, he had found when he believed the message of God's Word about what Jesus had done to save sinners. For several years he was a regular correspondent of mine until the Lord took him home—

a joyous saint whose doubts and fears had all been banished when he rested on the sure Word of God. His was the full assurance of faith.

Emotional Element in Conversion

And please do not misunderstand me. I do not discount the emotional element in conversion, but I insist it will not do to rely upon it as an evidence that one has been forgiven. When a man is awakened by the Spirit of God to realize something of his lost, undone condition, it would be strange indeed if his emotions were not aroused. When he is brought to repentance, that is, to a complete change of attitude toward his sins, toward himself, and toward God, we need not be surprised to see the tears of penitence coursing down his cheeks. And when he rests his soul on what God has said, and receives in faith the Spirit's witness, "Their sins and iniquities will I remember no more," it would be unthinkable but that, like Wesley, his heart should be strangely warmed as he rejoiced in God's salvation.

But what I am trying to make plain is that assurance is not based upon any emotional change, but whatever emotional experience there may be, it will be the result of accepting the testimony of the Lord given in the Scriptures. Faith rests on the naked Word of God. That Word believed gives full assurance. Then the Holy Spirit comes to dwell in the believer's heart and to conform him to Christ. Growth in grace follows naturally when the soul has trusted Christ and entered into peace with God.

Soon as my all I ventured
On the atoning blood,
The Holy Spirit entered
And I was born of God.

5

FULL ASSURANCE
OF UNDERSTANDING

W HEN WRITING to the Christians at Colosse, who had been saved largely through the ministry of Epaphras, that man of prayer and devotion, the Apostle Paul said: "For I would that ye knew what great conflict I have for you, and for them at Laodicea, and for as many as have not seen my face in the flesh; that their hearts might be comforted, being knit together in love, and unto all riches of the full assurance of understanding, to the acknowledgment of the mystery of God and of the Father, and of Christ; in whom are hid all the treasures of wisdom and knowledge" (Col. 2:1-3). The expression I desire to draw particular attention to is found in the second verse: "the full assurance of understanding."

The initial question of salvation having been settled, one is not to suppose that there will never arise any further doubts or perplexities. The child of God is a stranger and a pilgrim passing through an unfriendly wilderness-world, where he is beset by many foes who will seek in every way possible to impede his progress. He still has an enemy within—the old fleshy nature which is in constant warfare with the spiritual nature imparted in new birth.

Then outside, our adversary, the devil, goeth about
as a roaring lion, seeking whom he may devour. We
are called upon to resist him, being steadfast in the
faith. He knows he can never destroy the life hid with
Christ in God, but he will do everything that satanic
ingenuity can suggest to hinder the believer's progress
in spirituality and retard his growth in grace. By fiery
darts of doubt and incitements to carnal pleasure, he
will endeavor to hinder communion with God and so
to destroy the Christian's happiness and annul his testimony. Therefore the need of being built up on our
most holy faith and nurtured in sound scriptural instruction. "Through thy precepts," says David, "I get
understanding."

As soon as one knows he is saved, he should begin,
in dependence upon the Holy Spirit, a careful, regular,
systematic study of the Word of God. The Bible is our
Father's letter to us, His redeemed children. We should
value it as that which reveals His mind and indicates
the way in which He would have us walk. "All scripture is given by inspiration of God, and is profitable
for doctrine, for reproof, for correction, for instruction
in righteousness: that the man of God may be perfect,
throughly furnished unto all good works" (II Tim.
3:16-17). The study of the Word will instruct me in
the truth, it will show me what needs to be rectified in
my life and walk, it will make clear how I may get
right with God, and it will guide me in paths of up-
rightness. No Christian can afford to neglect his Bible.
If he does, he will be stunted and dwarfed in his
spiritual life, and will be a prey to doubts and fears,
and may be carried about by every wind of doctrine.

The Newborn Irishman

As newborn babes require milk, so the regenerated soul needs to be nourished on the Word. I wonder if you have heard the story of the Irishman who was converted through reading the New Testament. Rejoicing in his newfound treasure, he delighted to pore over its sacred pages whenever opportunity permitted.

One day the parish priest called to see him and found him perusing the precious volume that had brought such blessing to his soul.

"Pat," he asked sternly, "what book is that which you are reading?"

"Sure, yer riverance," was the reply, "it's the New Testament."

"The New Testament! Why, Pat, that's not a book for an ignorant man like you to read. That is for the clergy who go to college and learn its real meaning and then give it to the people. But unlearned folks like you will get all kinds of wrong ideas from it."

"But, yer riverance," said Pat, "I've just been reading here, and it's the blessed Apostle Peter himself that says it, 'As newborn babes, desire the sincere milk of the word, that ye may grow thereby,' and sure it's just a babe in Christ I am, and it's the milk of the Word I'm afther, and that's why I am reading it fer meself."

"That's all right, Pat, in a way, but the Almighty has appointed His priests to be the milkmen, and when you want the milk of the Word you should come to me and I will give it to you as you are able to bear it."

"Oh, sure, yer riverance, you know I kape a cow o' my own out there in the shed, and whin I was sick I hired a man to milk her fer me, and I soon found he

was shtealin' half the milk an' fillin' the bucket up with
wather. But whin I got well I discharged him and took
to milkin' me own cow, and now it's the rich cream
I'm gettin' all the time. And, yer riverance, whin I
depended on you fer the milk of the Word, man it
was the milk an' water stuff ye gave me, so now I'm
milkin' me own cow in this case, too, and it's the rich
cream o' the Word on which my soul is feedin' every
day."

Nothing will make up for lack of this diligent study
of the Bible for yourself. You cannot get the full
assurance of understanding without it. But as you
search the Scriptures you will find truth after truth
unfolding in a wonderful way, so that doubts and
questions will be banished and divinely given certainty
will take their place.

Discouraged Christians

Many uninstructed believers become discouraged because of their own failures and Satan takes advantage
of these to inject into their minds doubts as to whether
they are not deceiving themselves after all in supposing
they are Christians. But a knowledge of the truth as
to the believer's two natures will often help here. It is
important to understand that sin in the flesh, inherent
in the old nature, is not destroyed when one is born
again. On the contrary, that old sin principle remains
in the believer as long as he is in the body. What takes
place at new birth is that a new and divine nature is
communicated. These two natures are in conflict with
each other.

But the Christian who walks in the Spirit will not fulfill the desires of the flesh, even though at times those desires may be manifested. In order to so walk, one must take sides with God against this principle of evil which belongs to the old Adamic nature. God reckons it as executed at the cross of Christ, for the Lord Jesus died, not only for what we have done but for what we are by nature. Now faith accepts this as true, and the believer can exclaim, "I am crucified with Christ: nevertheless I live; yet not I, but Christ liveth in me: and the life that I now live in the flesh [that is, in the body] I live by the faith of the Son of God who loved me, and gave himself for me" (Gal. 2:20).

Carefully consider what is taught here: I, the responsible I, the old man, all that I was as a man in the flesh, including my entire sinful nature, *I* have been crucified with Christ. When was that? It was when Jesus died on Calvary's tree nineteen hundred years ago. He was there for me. I was there in Him. He was my Representative, my Substitute. He died the death I deserved to die. Therefore in God's eyes His death was my death. So I have died with Him.

Now I am called upon to make this real in my personal experience. I am to reckon myself as dead indeed unto sin, but alive unto God (Rom. 6:11). The old nature has no claim upon me. If it asserts itself and endeavors to bring me into bondage, I am to take sides with God against it. He has condemned sin in the flesh. I must condemn it too. Instead of yielding to it, I am to yield myself unto God as one alive from the dead, for I have been crucified in Christ's crucifixion, but I live anew in His resurrection. I am quick-

ened together with Christ, who Himself lives in me. He
then is my new Master. He is to take charge of me
and to control me for His glory. As yielded to Him,
I am freed from sin. "Sin shall not have dominion
over you: for ye are not under law, but under grace"
(Rom. 6:14). The sweet, constraining power of grace
leads me to present my body a living sacrifice, holy,
acceptable unto God, my intelligent service (Rom.
12:1).

Actually, I am still in the body, but I belong to the
new creation of which the risen Christ is the Head. It is
only the failure to recognize and act upon this that will
keep me from a life of victory.

Paul was eager for the Colossian and Laodicean believers to realize their place and responsibility in this
new creation. He tells them that he literally agonized
in spirit that they might apprehend this truth, and so
by heart occupation with Christ find complete deliverance from the power of the world, the flesh, and the
devil. He shows them that Christ Himself is the anti-
dote for human philosophy, legality, ritualism, and
asceticism, to all of which man is prone to turn when
seeking deliverance from the power of sin, but none
of which are of any real use against the indulgence
of the flesh.

It is occupation with a risen, glorified Saviour, our
exalted Head in heaven, that gives the victory we
crave. As risen with Him, we are exhorted to seek
the things which are above, where Christ sits on God's
right hand. "For ye died, and your life [your real life
as a new creature] is hid with Christ in God" (Col.
3:3, RV).

Another Irishman Shouts "Glory"

I have told of one Irishman who found his joy in the Word of God. Let me tell you of another who got the full assurance of understanding when he learned the truth I have been trying to unfold. He had been soundly converted. He knew he was saved and for a time was filled with joy thereby. But one day the awful thought came, "What if I should sin in such a way as to lose all this, and be lost myself after all?" He felt it would be unspeakably dreadful to have once known the Lord and then to fall from that high place of privilege, and so be overwhelmed in eternal woe. He brooded on this day and night, and was in great distress. But one evening in a meeting he heard the words read from Colossians 3:1-4, to which I have referred. I give them in full here: "If ye then be risen with Christ, seek those things which are above, where Christ sitteth on the right hand of God. Set your affection on things above, not on things on the earth. For ye are dead, and your life is hid with Christ in God. When Christ, who is our life, shall appear, then shall ye also appear with him in glory."

As these precious verses fell on his ears and he followed them with his eyes, something of their blessed certainty gripped his soul, and forgetting he was in a public gathering, he shouted aloud to the astonishment of those about him, "Glory to God! Whoiver heard of a man droundin' wid his head that high above water!"

You may smile at his apparent crudity of conception, but he had seen the truth that gives the full assurance of understanding. He realized his union with

Christ, and saw that since his Head was already in heaven he was eternally secure. Oh, what a soul-delivering truth this is! How it frees from self-occupation and how it glorifies Christ!

The practical outcome of it is seen in the verses that follow (Col. 3:5-17), where we are exhorted to mortify (that is, to put in the place of death, practically) our members which are upon the earth, judging every unclean and unholy propensity as having no place in the new creation, and therefore not to be tolerated for a moment as that which is ignoble and base. Then we are told what habits and behavior we are to put off, as discarded clothes that are unworthy of the new man; and we are directed what to put on as properly characteristic of a man in Christ. Please read the chapter for yourself.

The Lord Jesus said, "Ye shall know the truth, and the truth shall make you free." How necessary then for His redeemed ones to study His Word in dependence upon His Holy Spirit, that they may be delivered both from the fears that are the result of ignorance of His truth and the pride that is a result of self-confidence. The liberating Word alone will give to the honest, yielded soul who searches it prayerfully, in order that it shall have its sway over his life, the full assurance of understanding, for it is written: "The entrance of thy words giveth light; it giveth understanding unto the simple."

Go On! Go On! Go On!

And so as one goes on in the Christian life, and various problems and perplexities arise, it will be found

that the Word of God will give the answer to them all,
so far as it is His will that we should understand them
down here. There will always be mysteries beyond our
comprehension, for God's ways are not our ways, and
His thoughts are not our thoughts. But the trusting
soul learns to be content with what He has revealed,
and so to quietly leave the rest to be unfolded in that
coming day when we shall behold Him as He is, and
in His light shall see light, and know even as we ourselves are known of Him.

> When I shall wake in that fair morn of morns,
> After whose dawning never night returns,
> And with whose glory day eternal burns,
>   I shall be satisfied.
>
> When I shall meet with those that I have loved,
> Clasp in my arms the dear ones long removed,
> And find how faithful Thou to me hast prov'd,
>   I shall be satisfied.

Until then, the Word is to be a lamp unto our feet
and a light unto our path, whereby we walk safely
and securely through a world where sin and sorrow
reign, and where there are inscrutable mysteries on
every hand, unsolvable by human intelligence, knowing that all is well for those who are known of God
and are the called according to His purpose of grace as
revealed in Christ Jesus. Enough has been set forth
in His Word to give our hearts rest, and to keep our
souls in peace as we enjoy the "full assurance of understanding." The rest we can leave to Him who doeth
all things well, and who loves us with an everlasting
love.

I am not skilled to understand
What God hath will'd, what God hath plann'd;
I only know at His right hand
   Is One who is my Saviour!

I take Him at His word indeed:
"Christ died for sinners," this I read;
For in my heart I find a need
   Of Him to be my Saviour!

6

FULL ASSURANCE OF HOPE

ONE OF THE LITERATI of this world has told us that "hope springs eternal in the human breast." Regarding some phases of life this may be true, but concerning the eternal future the Word of God tells us that in our unregenerate state we were in a hopeless condition. In Ephesians 2:11-12, we read: "Wherefore remember, that ye being in time past Gentiles in the flesh, who are called Uncircumcision by that which is called the Circumcision in the flesh made by hands; that at that time ye were without Christ, being aliens from the commonwealth of Israel, and strangers from the covenants of promise, having no hope, and without God in the world."

But when one trusts in Christ all this is changed. From that moment on, the believer has a "good hope through grace." In Romans 8:24-25, we are told: "For we are saved by hope: but hope that is seen is not hope: for what a man seeth, why doth he yet hope for? But if we hope for that we see not, then do we with patience wait for it."

Note, this does not say we hope to be saved, but we *are saved* by, or perhaps more properly, in hope. He who has the full assurance of faith and of understanding, and knows on the authority of the word of Him who cannot lie that he is already justified and eternally saved now, has the hope set before him of the redemption of his body at the return of the Lord Jesus, when he will be conformed fully to the image of God's Son. This hope buoys him up as he faces the manifold trials and vicissitudes of life, and gives him courage to endure as seeing Him who is invisible.

The opening section of the fifth chapter of Romans may be pertinently quoted here (vv. 1-5): "Therefore being justified by faith, we have peace with God through our Lord Jesus Christ: by whom also we have access by faith into this grace wherein we stand, and rejoice in hope of the glory of God. And not only so, but we glory in tribulations also: knowing that tribulation worketh patience; and patience, experience; and experience, hope: and hope maketh not ashamed; because the love of God is shed abroad in our hearts by the Holy Ghost which is given unto us."

We have already seen that our assurance is not based upon an emotional experience, but on a "Thus saith the Lord." But we should by no means belittle experience. The renewed man enjoys true Christian experience which is produced by the knowledge of Christ as the One who undertakes for him in all the varied trials of the way. These are designed by God to work together for the perfecting of Christian character. It is therefore a great mistake to shrink from trouble, or to pray to be kept free from tribulation.

Praying for Patience

The story has often been told of the younger Christian who sought the counsel and help of an older brother, a minister of Christ. "Pray for me," he entreated, "that I may be given more patience." Down on their knees they dropped and the minister pleaded with God, "O Lord, send this brother more tribulations and trials!"

"Hold," exclaimed the other, "I did not ask you to pray that I might have tribulations but patience."

"I understood you," was the reply, "but we are told in the Word that 'tribulation worketh patience.' "

It is a lesson most of us are slow to learn. But note the steps as given in the passage above: tribulation, patience, experience, hope; and so the soul is unashamed, basking in the enjoyment of the divine love shed abroad in the heart by the Holy Spirit who dwells within.

With this before us, it ought to be easy to understand what is meant when in Hebrews 6:10-12 we read of "the full assurance of hope." "For God is not unrighteous to forget your work and labor of love, which ye have showed toward his name, in that ye have ministered to the saints and do minister. And we desire that every one of you do show the same diligence to the full assurance of hope unto the end: that ye be not slothful, but followers of them who through faith and patience inherit the promises."

As one walks with God, and learns to suffer and endure as seeing Him who is invisible, eternal things become more real than the things of time and sense, which are everything to the merely natural man. Thus there comes to the heart a trustful calm, a full assurance, based not alone upon the revealed Word but upon a personal knowledge of communion with God, which gives implicit confidence as to this present life and all that lies ahead.

One was once asked, "How do you know that Jesus lives—that He has actually been raised from the dead?"

"Why," was the answer, "I have just come from a half-hour interview with Him. I know I cannot be mistaken."

And this testimony might be multiplied by millions who, through all the Christian centuries, have borne witness to the reality of the personal companionship of Christ Jesus by the Spirit, drawing out the heart in love and devotion, and answering prayer in such a way as to make it impossible to doubt His tender care.

The Young Man Convinced

The late Robert T. Grant told me that on one occasion, while traveling, he was sitting in the Pullman reading his Bible, and he noticed the people around; many with nothing to do. He opened up his bag and got out some gospel tracts, and after distributing them he sat down again. A young man left his own seat and moved over to the preacher, and asked, "What did you give this to me for?"

"Why, it is a message from heaven for you, to give you rest in your soul," replied Mr. Grant.

The young man sneered and said, "I used to believe in that stuff years ago, but when I went to school and got educated, I threw it all overboard. I found out there's nothing to it."

"Will you let me read to you something I was going over just a moment ago?" Mr. Grant asked. " 'The

LORD is my shepherd: I shall not want.' Is there nothing in that, young man? I have known the blessedness of that for many years. Is there nothing in it?"

The young man replied, "Go on, read what comes next."

" 'He maketh me to lie down in green pastures: he leadeth me beside the still waters. He restoreth my soul: he leadeth me in the paths of righteousness for his name's sake.' Is there nothing in that?"

"Pardon me, sir, let me hear some more," said the young man.

" 'Yea, though I walk through the valley of the shadow of death, I will fear no evil: for thou art with me; thy rod and thy staff they comfort me.' Is there nothing in that?"

Then the young man cried, "Oh, forgive me, sir, there is everything in that! My mother died with those words upon her lips and besought me to trust her Saviour, but I have gotten far away from Him. You have brought it all back. Tell me more."

And as God's servant opened up the truth as to the way of salvation, the young man who had been so careless and unbelieving was convicted of his sin, and led to trust in Christ and confess Him as His own Saviour right there in that Pullman car.

Yes, there is everything in the blessed companionship of Christ, the Lord, both in life and in death, and it is this that gives the full assurance of hope.

But, unhappily, this assurance may become clouded and in a measure lost by spiritual negligence and carelessness in regard to prayer and feeding upon the Word. Therefore the need of such an exhortation as we have before us, which urges us to "show the same diligence to the full assurance of hope unto the end."

The Unhappy Backslider

Peter speaks of some who through waywardness have gotten so far out of fellowship with God that they have forgotten that they were purged from their old sins. This is a sad state to be in. It is what is commonly called in the Old Testament "backsliding." "The backslider in heart shall be filled with his own devices" (Prov. 14:14). An old preacher I knew as a boy used to say, "Backsliding always begins in the knee." And this is very true indeed. Neglect of prayer will soon dull the keen edge of one's spiritual sensibilities, and make it easy for a believer to drift into worldliness and carnality, as a result of which his soul's eyesight will become dimmed and he will lose the heavenly vision.

The backslider is shortsighted. He sees the things of this poor world very vividly, but he cannot see afar off, as he could in the days of his former, happy state. To such comes the exhortation, "Anoint thine eyes with eyesalve, that thou mayest see." Get back to your Bible and back to your knees. Let the Holy Spirit reveal to your penitent heart the point of departure where you left your first love, and judge it definitely before God. Acknowledge the sins and failures that have caused eternal things to lose their preciousness. Cry with David, as you confess your wanderings, "Restore unto me the joy of thy salvation." And He who is married to the backslider will give you again to know the blessedness of fellowship with Himself, and once more your peace will flow as a river and the full assurance of hope be yours.

As you walk with God your faith will grow exceedingly, your love unto all saints will be greatly enlarged, and the hope laid up for you in heaven will fill the vision of your opened eyes, as your heart is occupied with the Lord Himself who has restored your soul.

For it is well to remember that He Himself is our hope. He has gone back to the Father's house to prepare a place for us and He has promised to come again to receive us unto Himself, that where He is we may be also.

This is a purifying hope. In I John 3:1-3 the Spirit of God tells us so: "Behold, what manner of love the Father hath bestowed upon us, that we should be called the sons of God: therefore the world knoweth us not, because it knew him not. Beloved, now are we the sons of God, and it doth not yet appear what we shall be: but we know that, when he shall appear, we shall be like him; for we shall see him as he is. And every man that hath this hope in him purifieth himself, even as he is pure." The third verse has been translated, "Every man that hath this hope set on him, purifieth himself," etc. As we are occupied, not with the signs of the times, or simply with prophetic truth, but with the coming One who is our hope, we must of necessity become increasingly like Him. We shall learn to hate the things that He cannot approve, and so, cleansing ourselves from all filthiness of the flesh and spirit, we shall seek to be perfected in holiness as we await His imminent return.

So with this hope to cheer us,
And with the Spirit's seal
That all our sins are pardoned
Through Him whose stripes did heal;
As strangers and as pilgrims,
No place on earth we own,
But wait and watch as servants
Until our Lord shall come.

This hope will be the mainspring of our loyalty to Him whom we long to see. We are exhorted to be "like servants who wait for their Lord," and are occupied for Him, that whether He come at morn, at noon or at night, we may be ready always to meet Him, and so not be ashamed before Him at His coming. "Blessed is that servant, whom his lord when he cometh shall find so doing" (Matt. 24:46).

No wonder this is called a "blessed hope," as in Titus 2:11-14: "For the grace of God that bringeth salvation hath appeared to all men, teaching us that, denying ungodliness and worldly lusts, we should live soberly, righteously, and godly, in this present world; looking for that blessed hope, and the glorious appearing of the great God and our Saviour Jesus Christ; who gave himself for us, that he might redeem us from all iniquity, and purify unto himself a peculiar people, zealous of good works."

The Great School of Grace

It is not merely that we are now saved by grace, but we are also in the school of grace, here to learn how to behave ourselves in such a manner as to have the constant approval of Him who has made us His own. And so grace is here presented as our instructor, teaching us the importance of the denial of self, and the refusal of all that is contrary to the mind of God, in order that we may manifest by clean and holy lives the reality of the faith that we profess, while we have ever before our souls that blessed hope of the appearing of the glory of our great God and Saviour Jesus Christ.

At His first coming He died to redeem us from all lawlessness, that He might purify us unto Himself a people of His own possession, zealously engaged in all good works. At His second coming He will redeem our bodies and make us wholly like Himself in all things. What a wonderful hope this is, and as we live in the power of it what assurance we have of the unchanging love of Him whose face we soon shall see!

Often when the dead in Christ are being laid away, we are reminded that we commit their precious bodies to the grave "in the sure and certain hope of a glorious resurrection." And this is a most blessed truth. For when the hope of the Lord's return is realized, the saints of all past ages who died in faith will share with those who may be alive upon the earth at that time, in the wonderful change that will then take place when "the Lord himself shall descend from heaven with a shout, with the voice of the archangel, and with the trump of God: and the dead in Christ shall rise first: then we which are alive and remain shall be caught up together with them in the clouds, to meet the Lord in the air: and so shall we ever be with the Lord" (I Thess. 4:16-17). How bright a hope is this and who knows how soon it may be realized! Let us not falter, nor give way to doubt or unbelief, but give diligence in maintaining "the full assurance of hope" until it gives place to full realization.

Often we may feel that "hope deferred maketh the heart sick," but the consummation is sure. Meantime let us be busy in our Master's service, and particularly in trying to win others, bringing them to share with us in the joy of God's salvation. When at last our little day of service here is ended, not one of us will feel that we have given up too much for Christ, or be sorry that we have labored too earnestly for His glory; but, I fear, many of us would then give worlds, were they ours, if we could only go back to earth and live our lives over again, in sincerity and unselfishness, seeking alone the honor of Him who has redeemed us.

It is better to be saved so as by fire than not to be saved at all, but surely none of us would desire to meet our Master empty-handed, but the rather to "come with rejoicing" into His presence, when our hope is fulfilled, bringing our sheaves with us. Let us then remember that we have

> Only a little while to tell the wondrous story
>   Of Him who made our guilt and curse His own:
> Only a little while till we behold His glory,
>   And sit with Him upon His throne.

And so may we ever heed His command, "Occupy till I come."

7

ASSURANCE UNTO ALL MEN

IN THE LAST ANALYSIS, the real basic ground for this assurance, not only of the individual salvation of each believer but of the eventual carrying out of the divine program in its entirety, rests solely upon the resurrection of our Lord Jesus Christ. This is emphasized by the Apostle Paul in his great sermon addressed to the Athenian philosophers on Mars Hill, as recorded in Acts 17. There, after pointing out the unreasonableness and wicked folly of idolatry, he declared the truth as to the Unknown God, the Creator of heaven and earth, and added: "And the times of this ignorance God winked at; but now commandeth all men everywhere to repent: because he hath appointed a day, in which he will judge the world in righteousness by that man whom he hath ordained; whereof he hath given assurance unto all men, in that he hath raised him from the dead" (Acts 17:30-31).

He had himself received ocular proof of that resurrection of which he spoke. The risen Christ had appeared to him, as he fell to the ground on the Damascus road, overcome by a supernatural light from heaven. And at this very time there were living many witnesses of the greatest miracle of all the ages, for when writing to the Corinthian church, some years later than his visit to Athens, he enumerated over five hundred who could bear positive testimony to the resurrection of our Lord, "of whom," he added, "the greater part remain unto this present, but some are fallen asleep" (I Cor. 15:5-6).

Horace Bushnell declared that the resurrection of Jesus Christ is the best attested fact of ancient history. Think of the authoritative sources for any other outstanding event, and compare them with the proofs of the resurrection, and you will realize the fairness of this remark.

The writers of the four Gospels were men of the sincerest piety and probity, as their works attest. They unite in giving unqualified testimony to the resurrection of Christ. The other New Testament writers—Paul, James, Peter, and Jude—definitely mention or clearly imply the same glorious fact. They all speak of Christ Jesus as the living One, who once died for our sins. Concerning what other ancient historical event can the testimony of so many eyewitnesses be cited?

Even the enemies of the gospel bore unwilling witness to the resurrection by their clumsy efforts to interpret to their advantage the empty sepulcher on that first Easter Sunday. They knew Jesus had predicted that He would rise again in three days, and so they went to Pilate demanding that steps be taken to prevent His disciples from stealing the body of their Master. Pilate gave them a guard and commanded the sealing of the tomb, and grimly added, "Make it as sure as ye can!" But all their efforts were in vain. When the appointed hour struck, angelic hands broke the Roman imperial seal and rolled back the stone, revealing an empty crypt—the body was not there. Certainly none of His foes rifled that grave. They were determined to keep the body of Jesus there as long as time should last. And if they could have produced that body later, in order to disprove the message of the resurrection, certainly they would have done so.

And it is preposterous to credit the story circulated by the wily priesthood that His disciples came by night, and stole away His body, for even they "knew not the scripture, that he must rise from the dead." The amazing thing is that His enemies remembered what His friends had forgotten. The empty tomb was as great a shock to those who loved Jesus, as it was a fearful portent to those who hated Him.

Christ's Bodily Resurrection Real

Only the personal appearances of the risen Christ convinced them of the reality of His resurrection. The forty days during which He appeared to them on many occasions, instructing them concerning the kingdom of God, furnished ample proof that He had really triumphed over death, and this glorious fact gave them that confidence which enabled them to stand against all opposition, witnessing to every man that God had raised His body from the grave. They beheld Him as He was taken up from them into heaven in that same body, and after receiving the Pentecostal enduement, they went about bearing witness to the resurrection of their Lord with great power.

This is the outstanding message of the church. He

who died for our sins lives again for our justification. The resurrection of the material body of flesh and bones is the proof that God is satisfied with the redemptive work of His Son. It declares that God can now be just and the Justifier of him who believes on the Lord Jesus. To say that though Christ is dead physically He is alive spiritually will not do. That might be true of any man. It would be no evidence of divine satisfaction in His work.

Some years ago an eloquent New York preacher, who denies the physical resurrection of the Saviour, declared, "The body of Jesus still sleeps in an unknown Syrian tomb, but His soul goes marching on!" Many applauded this as a wonderful explanation of the influence of Jesus down through the ages. But it is utterly false and fallacious. If the body of Jesus still rests in the grave, He was not what He professed to be and is powerless to save.

This heresy (for heresy it is) is not new. It became prevalent in certain circles even in apostolic days, as I Corinthians 15 proves. In the Corinthian church there were some who accepted the teaching of the Sadducees and denied the reality of a literal resurrection. Sternly, Paul challenges them in the well-known words: "Now if Christ be preached that he rose from the dead, how say some among you that there is no resurrection of the dead? But if there be no resurrection of the dead, then is Christ not risen: and if Christ be not risen, then is our preaching vain, and your faith is also vain. Yea, and we are found false witnesses of God; because we have testified of God that he raised up Christ: whom he raised not up, if so be that the dead rise not. For if the dead rise not, then is not Christ raised: and if Christ be not raised, your faith is vain; ye are yet in your sins. Then they also which are fallen asleep in Christ are perished. If in this life only we have hope in Christ, we are of all men most miserable" (I Cor: 15:12-19).

Here is sturdy logic indeed, and withal inspired by the Holy Spirit. If Christ be not risen we have no gospel to preach, and there is no message of deliverance for poor, lost sinners held captive in chains of iniquity. Faith in a dead Christ will not save anyone. The gospel is the dynamic of God unto salvation because it proclaims a living, loving Redeemer who is waiting to manifest His power on behalf of all who trust in Him.

What the Resurrection of Christ Attests

Let us then notice carefully what the Word of God tells us about this glorious truth.

1. The resurrection of the Lord Jesus attests the truthfulness of His claims concerning His divine person and mission. To His enemies He said, "Destroy this temple, and in three days I will raise it up." But He spoke of the temple of His body. To His disciples He declared, "No man taketh it [my life] from me, but I lay it down of myself. I have power to lay it down, and to take it again. This commandment have I received of my Father." He definitely told them that the Son of man must be betrayed into the hands of sinners, and He added, "They shall scourge him, and put him to death: and the third day he shall rise again" (Luke 18:33).

Therefore if He failed to come out of the tomb in a resurrected, physical body of flesh and bones, all that He claimed regarding Himself and His saving power was invalidated. But He did not fail! It was not possible that He would be held by death. He fulfilled His word by rising again on the third day.

2. His resurrection attests the truth of the prophetic scriptures. The Old Testament abounds in prophecies of Messiah's death and resurrection. In Psalm 16, David foretold concerning Him, "Thou wilt not leave my soul in hell [Sheol, or Hades, the abode of the dead]; neither wilt thou suffer thine Holy One to see corruption." Both Peter and Paul show us that this passage had its fulfillment in the resurrection of Christ.

Isaiah wrote seven hundred years before His birth, "When thou shalt make his soul an offering for sin, he shall see his seed, he shall prolong his days, and the pleasure of the LORD shall prosper in his hand" (Isa. 53:10). Here is a remarkable statement. Death was not to end the activities of Jehovah's Servant. After He had given His life as an oblation for sin, He was to prolong His days, and so in resurrection be the Administrator of God's great plan for the blessing of mankind.

3. The resurrection of the Lord Jesus was the display of omnipotent power on our behalf. In Ephesians 1:17-23 we have the apostle's prayer for all believers. He asks that the eyes of their hearts might be opened, in order that they might know the hope of His calling, the riches of the glory of His inheritance in the saints and the "exceeding greatness of his power to us-ward who believe, according to the working of his mighty

power, which he wrought in Christ when he raised him from the dead." The same mighty energy that was put forth to revivify the body of Jesus, and raise Him from among the dead, is the power that quickens dead souls into newness of life and energizes children of God so as to enable them to live even on earth a heavenly life of victory over sin, while they walk in fellowship with Him under the control of His Holy Spirit.

4. The resurrection of Christ is the proof that the sin question has been settled to God's satisfaction. On the cross our sins were laid upon Him. He voluntarily accepted responsibility for them. He bore them in His own body on the tree. "He was delivered for our offences, and was raised again for [or, on account of] our justification" (Rom. 4:25). When God raised His Son from death it was His way of expressing His recognition of the perfection of His finished work. If sin had not been forever put away, He would never have come forth from that grave; but having paid for us the uttermost farthing, death had no claim upon Him. By raising Him God declared to all created intelligences His full approval of and His acceptance of the work of His blessed Son.

5. Christ's resurrection is therefore the believing sinner's assurance that his record is now clear. God Himself has no charge against him who puts his trust in Jesus. So we read in Romans 8:32-34: "He that spared not his own Son, but delivered him up for us all, how shall he not with him also freely give us all things? Who shall lay anything to the charge of God's elect? It is God that justifieth. Who is he that con-

demneth? It is Christ that died, yea rather, that is risen again, who is even at the right hand of God, who also maketh intercession for us." Observe that no voice can now be raised to condemn the one who rests in Christ's finished work. His death and resurrection effectually forbid the raising of the sin question again, as far as any believer is concerned. The resurrection is like a receipt for full payment made. On the cross the mighty debt we owed was settled. A risen Christ tells us that every claim has been met and God holds nothing against the believer.

> Now we see in Christ's acceptance
> But the measure of our own,
> He who lay beneath our sentence
> Seated high upon the throne.

6. His resurrection is the token that through Him God will judge the world. That judgment is based on man's attitude toward the One whom the Father delights to honor. If men receive Him as Lord and Saviour they will never have to come into judgment for their sins, because He was judged in their room and stead. But if men refuse Him and spurn His grace, they will not only have to answer before Him for all their sins, but in addition to all the rest, they will be judged for rejecting Him who died to save them.

7. It is His resurrection which alone gives validity to the gospel message and delivers the believer from the fear of death. Turning now to II Timothy 1:8-10, we read this important admonition: "Be not thou therefore ashamed of the testimony of our Lord, nor of me his prisoner: but be thou partaker of the afflictions of the gospel according to the power of God; who

hath saved us, and called us with an holy calling, not according to our works, but according to his own purpose and grace, which was given us in Christ Jesus before the world began, but is now made manifest by the appearing of our Saviour Jesus Christ, who hath abolished death, and hath brought life and immortality to light through the gospel."

Do not, I beg of you, read these words carelessly. Go over them again and again, until their force and their solemnity and their preciousness have gripped your soul. Our entire salvation hangs on the truth that our Saviour, Jesus Christ, has abolished (that is, annulled the power of) death, and has brought life and immortality to light through the gospel. He went down into the dark stream of death. All its waves and billows rolled over Him. But He came up in resurrection life never to die again. And so for us the waters of this Jordan have been rolled back, and there is a dry way through death for all who believe. Listen to His triumphant words, "I am the resurrection, and the life: he that believeth in me, though he were dead, yet shall he live: and whosoever liveth and believeth in me shall never die. Believeth thou this?" (John 11:25-26). Does not your heart reply, "Yes, Lord, I do believe; I rest my soul forevermore upon Thy sure testimony, and I confess Thee as my Saviour and my Lord"?

God's Assurance That Christ Arose

It is thus that God gives assurance unto all men in that He hath raised Christ from the dead. If Satan should try to discourage you by occupying you with your own unworthiness and your manifest short-

comings, do not attempt to argue with him, but look
up to the throne of God and there contemplate the
risen One who once hung a bleeding Victim on the
cross of shame, and whose lifeless body once lay in
Joseph's new tomb. Remember, He could not be
yonder in the glory if one sin remained unsettled.
Therefore, every believer can sing with assurance:

> The Lord is risen, with Him we also rose,
> And in His death see vanquished all our foes.
> The Lord is risen, we stand beyond the doom
> Of all our sins, through Jesus' empty tomb.

The young convert was right, who said, when this
truth was revealed to him by the Spirit: "If anyone
is ever to be kept out of heaven for my sins, it will
have to be Jesus, for He took them all upon Himself
and made Himself responsible for them. But He is in
heaven already, never to be turned out, so now I know
that I am secure as long as He lives, the One who
once died in my place." This expresses it exactly, for
faith is just saying "Amen" to what God has made
known in His Word. The believer sets to his seal that
God is true, and so rests everything for eternity on the
fact that Christ, who died for our sins on the cross
of shame, has been raised to endless life.

It is noticeable that the entire Trinity of the Godhead is concerned in this marvelous event, and each
divine Person participated in our Lord's rising from
the dead.

As we have already seen, His resurrection is attributed to Himself: "I lay down my life, that I might
take it again." Again He said, "Destroy this temple,
and in three days I will raise it up."

It is also attributed to the Father: "The God of peace, that brought again from the dead our Lord Jesus, that great shepherd of the sheep."

The Holy Spirit is likewise recognized as the direct Agent in bringing to pass this stupendous miracle: "But if the Spirit of him that raised up Jesus from the dead dwell in you, he that raised up Christ from the dead shall also quicken your mortal bodies by his Spirit that dwelleth in you."

And so each Person of the Godhead is concerned in proclaiming the testimony of Jesus and His resurrection to men and women everywhere—those who are dead in trespasses and sins, until quickened by the same mighty power that raised up our blessed Lord and set Him at God's right hand in the highest heaven.

Whoso hath felt the Spirit of the Highest,
   Cannot confound or doubt Him or deny:
Yea, with one voice, O world, though thou deniest,
   Stand then on *that* side, for on *this* am I.

8

ASSURANCE OF HEART

THERE IS A VERY PRECIOUS LINE of truth
unfolded in John's first epistle that has to do with the
experimental side of Christianity. In 3:18-19, we are
both exhorted and encouraged in the following words:
"My little children, let us not love in word, neither
in tongue; but in deed and in truth. And hereby we
know that we are of the truth, and shall assure our
hearts before him."

Now this assurance of heart is the result of the
Spirit's work in the believer, following the full assurance of faith. The moment I take God at His Word
and trust the Lord Jesus as my Saviour, I have eternal
life, and I know it on the authority of the Holy Scriptures, which over and over link the present possession
of this life with faith in the One whom God gave to
be the propitiation for our sins. And as I go on in the
Christian life I have abundant corroborative evidence
through the Holy Spirit's continuous work in my in-
most being that this is indeed far more than a doctrine
which I have accepted. I find from day to day positive
proofs that I am in very truth a new man, "created in
Christ Jesus unto good works, which God hath before
ordained that we should walk in them." Thus my assurance deepens. While at the beginning I rested every-

thing for eternity upon the naked Word of God, I find, as I continue in faith, overwhelming confirmation of the truth of that Word in the manifestations of eternal life actually imparted to me a sinner, through grace.

Let us look carefully at some of these corroborative proofs which assure our hearts before Him.

First, the believer becomes conscious of an inborn love for the will of God. "Hereby we do know that we know him, if we keep his commandments. He that saith, I know him and keepeth not his commandments, is a liar, and the truth is not in him. But whoso keepeth his word, in him verily is the love of God perfected; hereby know we that we are in him" (I John 2:3-5). It is not natural for the unbeliever to delight in the will of God. The unsaved man loves his own way and resents being asked to yield his will to another.

An English Barrister Counsels a Young Man

Mr. Montague Goodman, a well-known English barrister, who is also a widely recognized minister of Christ, recently related the following incident which will illustrate this point:

"Sitting in my study with me one evening was a young man whom I had known from his early boyhood. He was about to set out for the Far East and had come to say good-bye. We talked in a candid, friendly manner, and I sought to commend Christ to him. I shall not readily forget his reply. It was given without any trace of hostility or bitterness. He said, 'I want to do as I like. I don't see why I should surrender my liberty to Jesus Christ, or anybody else.'

"In so saying he was but expressing the mind of the whole race of which he was a member. For the universal truth concerning mankind is just this: 'We have turned everyone to his own way.' This is a man's condemnation before God; he is not prepared to subject himself to the will of God. He is set on having his own way, and resents any interference with it. He says in effect to God, 'Not Thy will, but mine be done.' He wills his own will, and this is universally true whether that will may be vulgar or refined, sensual or intellectual, honest or dishonest, cruel or kind. He claims the right to be the master of his fate, the captain of his soul."

But now consider what takes place at conversion. I trust in Christ as my Saviour and I own Him as my Lord. His all-embracing love wins my heart. I yield my will to His. Henceforth, however conscious I may be of daily failure, I find the supreme desire of my heart is to do as He would have me. I love His commandments. How truly Bonar's beautiful old hymn sets this forth:

> I was a wand'ring sheep,
>   I did not love the fold,
> I did not love my Shepherd's voice,
>   I would not be controlled;
> I was a wayward child,
>   I did not love my home,
> I did not love my Father's voice,
>   I loved afar to roam.
>
> The Shepherd sought His sheep,
>   The Father sought His child;
> He followed me o'er vale and hill,
>   O'er deserts waste and wild:

He found me nigh to death,
  Famished, and faint, and lone;
He bound me with the bands of love,
  He saved the wand'ring one.

Jesus my Shepherd is;
  'Twas He that loved my soul,
'Twas He that washed me in His blood,
  'Twas He that made me whole:
'Twas He that sought the lost,
  That found the wand'ring sheep;
'Twas He that brought me to the fold,
  'Tis He that still doth keep.

I was a wand'ring sheep,
  I would not be controlled,
But now I love my Shepherd's voice,
  I love, I love the fold:
I was a wayward child,
  I once preferred to roam;
But now I love my Father's voice,
  I love, I love His home!

A Changed Attitude Gives Assurance

This change of attitude gives me heart assurance that I am now a child of God by a second birth. Nothing else can properly explain the subduing of my once proud will, and my earnest desire to obey the commandments of God as set forth in His Word.

I hope none will be so foolish as to suppose that John's use of the word "commandments" has reference simply to the ten words given at Sinai. It goes far beyond that. The righteousness of the law is fulfilled in us, who walk not after the flesh, but after the Spirit. But over and above this we have the commandments of our Lord Jesus Christ, embracing all that He taught while He was here on earth as to the behavior of His

disciples; and also that which He has since revealed
by His Spirit, as set forth in the New Testament Scriptures. The regenerated man longs to do those things that
please his Lord; and as he walks in obedience, that
divine love which was shown in all its perfection at the
cross wells up in his own heart, as Christ becomes
increasingly precious the better He is known.

In the second instance, let us consider what is written in I John 3:9: "Whosoever is born of God doth
not commit sin; for his seed remaineth in him: and he
cannot sin, because he is born of God." This has puz-
zled many a careless reader, and even some who are
more careful. Satan himself has used it to distress
God's dear children, when God meant it to comfort
sensitive, conscientious souls. The devil says to such
an one, "You know you are not sinless. You frequently
fail in thought and word and deed, therefore you commit sin, and so you cannot be a child of God." The
troubled mind is inclined to accept this as clear and
logical, even when the heart that has trusted Christ
rebels against it, and feels instinctively that there is
something wrong and fallacious in such reasoning.

It will help us to see that the tense of the verb here
is what has been called the "present continuous." It is
not a question of occasional, or even of frequent failure, bitterly lamented and grieved over. It rather im-
plies a course of behavior that is characteristic. With
this in mind it will be well to go back to verse 6 and
read the entire section as given in a critical translation: "Whosoever abideth in Him does not practice
sin; whosoever practiceth sin hath not seen Him, neither known Him. Little children, let no man deceive

you; he that practiceth righteousness is righteous, even as He is righteous. He that practiceth sin is of the devil; for the devil practiceth sin from the beginning. For this purpose the Son of God was manifested, that He might destroy [or annul] the works of the devil. Whosoever is born of God doth not practice sin, for His seed remaineth [or abideth] in him and he cannot be practicing sin, because he is born of God. In this the children of God are manifest and the children of the devil: whosoever doth not practice righteousness is not of God, neither he that loveth not his brother."

How Two Different Families Act

See how the two families, the unregenerated and the regenerated, are here depicted. Unsaved men practice sin. Whatever fine things there may be in their characters, as judged by the world's standards, they delight in having their own way. This is the essence of sin. "Sin is lawlessness." All careful scholars agree that this is a more correct translation than "Sin is the transgression of the law." We are told that "until the law sin was in the world," and although sin was not imputed as transgression because no written standard had yet been given, nevertheless sin manifested itself as self-will, or lawlessness, and was seen everywhere among fallen mankind. Lawlessness is the refusal of a person to submit his will to Another, even to God Himself, who has the right to claim his full obedience. In this the children of the devil show plainly the family to which they belong.

But with the believer it is otherwise. Turning to Christ he is born from above, as we have seen, and

thus possesses a new nature. This new nature abomi-
nates sin, and henceforth dominates his desires and his
thinking. Sin becomes detestable. He loathes himself
for the follies and iniquities of his past, and he yearns
after holiness. Energized by the Holy Spirit, his life
trend is changed. He practices righteousness. Though
ofttimes conscious of failure, the whole trend of his
life is altered. The will of God is his joy and delight.
And as he learns more and more the preciousness of
abiding in Christ, he grows in grace and in knowledge,
and realizes that divine power is given him to walk in
the path of obedience. His new nature finds joy in
surrendering to Jesus as Lord, and so sin ceases to be
characteristic of his life and character.

This leads us on to the third corroborative evidence
of the new birth. "We know that we have passed from
death unto life, because we love the brethren. He that
loveth not his brother abideth in death" (I John 3:14).

There is a difference between the love spoken of
here and a merely human affection. Two different
words are used to distinguish these two aspects of love
in the Greek New Testament. The word here chosen
by the Spirit is used throughout to designate a love
that is divinely imparted. It far surpasses mere natural
affection. It is implanted in us when we are born again.

What a marvelous thing is this love shed abroad in
our hearts by the Holy Spirit given unto us! It links
us to all saints everywhere. Instinctively the newly converted soul feels that he belongs to a new family and
he claims all such as are saved as his brethren and
sisters in Christ. Before the great change came, he
shrank from the company of Christians and preferred

to associate with worldlings. Now he seeks out fellow believers, like those of old, concerning whom we read, "and being let go, they went to their own company."

Line of Demarcation Becomes Evident

Nor is this a passing notion, for as the years go on the line of demarcation only becomes stronger. The world becomes less and less attractive, and the family of the redeemed becomes more and more precious. Love of the brethren is an abiding proof of the new life, and so the heart is assured before God. This love is a very practical thing. The true child of God cannot be content with loving in word or in tongue. He will manifest love in active benevolence and in gracious behavior. This truth is stressed everywhere throughout the first epistle of John. "Beloved, let us love one another: for love is of God; and everyone that loveth is born of God, and knoweth God" (4:7).

It is a remarkable fact, however, that after emphasizing these internal evidences of the new birth so clearly in the early part of his letter, the apostle comes back in the closing portions to the great outstanding truth that the surest proof of all is simple faith in the testimony of God. It is because the more conscientious a soul is, the more he will distrust himself and his experiences, and hence it will not do to build upon these experiences apart from the great foundation truths of the gospel.

So in I John 4:13-16 we are told: "Hereby know we that we dwell in him, and he in us, because he hath given us of his Spirit. And we have seen and do testify that the Father sent the Son to be the Saviour of the world. Whosoever shall confess that Jesus is the Son of God, God dwelleth in him, and he in God. And we have known and believed the love that God hath to us. God is love; and he that dwelleth in love dwelleth in God, and God in him."

Reading this, one might ask, "But how do I know that He has given the Spirit to me?" The answer is that it is the Spirit who bears witness to the eternal verities of the gospel. He indwells all who have trusted Christ as their personal Saviour. If you have done this and confess that Jesus is the Son of God, you may know that God by the Spirit dwells in you, and you in God. His love has been revealed in the gospel. Nature manifests His power and wisdom. It is the cross that tells of His love and grace. Dr. Horatius Bonar, one of whose well-known hymns we have quoted before, has brought this out most strikingly in another poem, not so widely known.

> We read Thee in the flowers, the trees,
> The freshness of the fragrant breeze,
> The songs of birds upon the wing,
> The joy of summer and of spring.
>
> We read Thee best in Him who came
> To bear for us the Cross of shame
> Sent by the Father from on high,
> Our life to live, our death to die.

When our Saviour had made purification for sins He was taken up into heaven and seated on God's right hand. The Holy Spirit then came down to earth to give power to the testimony of the work so blessedly accomplished, when the Roman spear pierced the side of the dead Christ, and "forthwith came there out blood and water." That blood and water bore mute witness to His holy life given up for sinners. To this the Spirit adds His divine record. And so, as we are informed in I John 5:8, "There are three who bear witness, the Spirit, and the water, and the blood: and the three agree in one" (RV).

Thus God has given abundant testimony to the perfection of the redemptive work of His Son. And now He calls on man to receive that testimony in faith and thus be eternally saved. We credit the testimony of men in whom we have confidence, even though they speak of matters beyond our knowledge or our ability to verify. Surely, then, we should accept unquestioningly the witness that God has given concerning His Son! To do otherwise, to refuse to trust His record, is to make Him a liar. To believe the record is to receive this divinely given message into the very heart and soul. Therefore John tells us, "He that believeth on the Son of God hath the witness in himself." And so John brings us back to that which we dwelt on in an earlier chapter of this book: "These things have I written unto you that believe on the name of the Son of God; that ye may know that ye have eternal life, even you who believe on the name of the Son of God" (I John 5:13, literal trans.).

It becomes evident, then, that the term "these things" embraces all that the venerable apostle has been setting before us in this epistle of light and love. Go over it again. Take it up point by point. Follow the Spirit's presentation of "the message" from verse to verse and theme to theme. Receive it as it is in truth the very Word of the living God, and know beyond

any cavil or doubt that you are born from above and
have everlasting life as a present possession. And so
your heart shall be assured before Him.

> Blessed assurance, Jesus is mine!
> O what a foretaste of glory divine!
> Heir of salvation, purchase of God,
> Born of His Spirit, washed in His blood.

PART II

1

DIFFICULTIES WHICH HINDER FULL ASSURANCE

I T IS NOW MY PURPOSE to consider some of the difficulties and perplexities which keep souls from entering into peace and enjoying the full assurance of salvation. These questions and objections are some that have come to me again and again from earnest seekers after light, and are therefore, I have good reason to believe, fairly representative of the troublesome thoughts that hinder many from seeing the simplicity of God's way of life, as set forth in His holy Word. Perhaps if my reader has not a settled rest of heart and conscience, he may find his own peculiar trouble dealt with here.

1. *"How may I be sure that I have repented enough?"*

Very often the real difficulty arises from a misapprehension of the meaning of repentance. There is no salvation without repentance, but it is important to see exactly what is meant by this term. It should not be confused with penitence, which is sorrow for sin;

nor with penance, which is an effort to make some satisfaction for sin; nor yet with reformation, which is turning from sin. Repentance is a change of attitude toward sin, toward self, and toward God. The original word (in the Greek Testament) literally means "a change of mind." This is not a mere intellectual change of viewpoint, however, but a complete reversal of attitude.

Now test yourself in this way. You once lived in sin and loved it. Do you now desire deliverance from it? You were once self-confident and trusting in your own fancied goodness. Do you now judge yourself as a sinner before God? You once sought to hide from God and rebelled against His authority. Do you now look up to Him, desiring to know Him, and to yield yourself to Him? If you can honestly say yes to these questions, you have repented. Your attitude is altogether different to what it once was.

You confess you are a sinner, unable to cleanse your own soul, and you are willing to be saved in God's way. This is repentance. And remember, it is not the amount of repentance that counts: it is the fact that you turn from self to God that puts you in the place where His grace avails through Jesus Christ.

Strictly speaking, not one of us has ever repented enough. None of us has realized the enormity of our guilt as God sees it. But when we judge ourselves and trust the Saviour whom He has provided, we are saved through His merits. As recipients of His lovingkindness, repentance will be deepened and will continue day by day, as we learn more and more of His infinite worth and our own unworthiness.

It is not thy tears of repentance, nor prayers,
    But the blood that atones for the soul;
On Him then who shed it thou mayest at once
    Thy weight of iniquities roll.

2. *"I do not feel fit for God; I am so unworthy, I fear He will not take me in."*

What a wretched condition would be yours if you imagined you were fit, in yourself, for heaven, or that you were worthy of such love as God has shown! It is because of your lack of fitness that Christ died to redeem you. It is because you are worthy only of eternal judgment that He "who knew no sin" was made sin for you, that you might become the righteousness of God in Him. If you had any fitness of your own, you would not need a Saviour.

When the Roman centurion sought the healing power of Jesus for his servant, he sent the Jewish elders to the Lord to intercede for him. They said, "He is worthy that thou shouldest do this for him; for he loveth our nation, and himself built us a synagogue." But when the centurion faced the Lord, he exclaimed, "I am not worthy that thou shouldest come under my roof."

They said, "He is worthy"; he declared, "I am not worthy," and this moved the heart of Jesus, so that He exclaimed, "I have not found so great faith, no, not in Israel."

So long as a man considers himself worthy there is no salvation for him; but when, in repentance, he owns his unworthiness, there is immediate deliverance for him through faith in the Lord Jesus Christ. With-

out repentance the sinner is unable to believe unto
salvation.

> Let not conscience make you linger,
>   Nor of fitness fondly dream;
> All the fitness He requireth,
>   Is to feel your need of Him.

3. *"I am afraid I am too great a sinner ever to be
   saved."*

But Christ came not to call the righteous, but sinners
to repentance. He did not die for good people, and in
truth there are no intrinsically good people in the
world. "There is none that doeth good, no, not one."
But if any imagine they are good in themselves, there
is no salvation for them. "They that are whole need not
a physician, but they that are sick." Sin is like a dire
disease that fastens upon the whole being, but Jesus is
the great Physician who cures the worst of cases. None
can be too vile, or too sinful, or too wicked for Him.
His skill is unlimited. He delights to show great grace
to great sinners. Saul of Tarsus was the chief of sinners,
but he was saved in that moment when he trusted the
Lord Jesus.

The greater your sinfulness, the more you need the
Saviour; and the worse your condition, the more proof
you have that you are the one for whom He died. God
laid all our sins upon His Son when He hung on that
cross of Calvary. He suffered for them all. Not one of
your sins was overlooked. There is such infinite value
in His propitiatory work that grace can now be ex-
tended to the vilest sinner on the face of the earth, if
he will but receive the Lord Jesus by faith as his personal Saviour.

My sin—oh, the bliss of this glorious thought—
   My sin—not in part but the whole,
Is nailed to His cross and I bear it no more,
   Praise the Lord, praise the Lord, oh, my soul!

4. *"But what if I am not one of the elect?"*

You can readily settle that yourself. Without attempting to delve into the mysteries of the divine decrees and the divine foreknowledge, it is enough to say that all who come to God through His Son are elect. Our Lord makes this very plain in John 6:37. He says, "All that the Father giveth me shall come to me; and him that cometh to me I will in no wise cast out." Now do not linger too long on the first half of the verse. Be clear about the latter half, for it is there that your responsibility is found. Have you come to Jesus? If so, you have His pledged word that He will not cast you out. The fact that you come proves that the Father gave you to Christ. Thus you may be certain that you belong to the glorious company of the elect.

D. L. Moody used to put it very simply: "The elect are the 'whosoever wills'; the non-elect are the 'whosoever won'ts.'" This is exactly what Scripture teaches. The invitation is to all. Those who accept it are the elect. Remember, we are never told that Christ died for the elect. But what does the Word say? "Christ died for the ungodly." Are you ungodly? Then He died for you. Put in your claim and enter into peace.

Meditate on the Holy Spirit's declaration through the Apostle Paul: "This is a faithful saying, and worthy of all acceptation, that Christ Jesus came into the world to save sinners; of whom I am chief." Nowhere are we told that Christ came to save the elect. The term "sinners" is all-embracing, for "all have sinned, and come short of the glory of God." Are you *sure* you are a sinner? Then you may be *certain* there is salvation for you. Do not exercise yourself in matters too high for you. Just be simple enough to take God at His word.

> Sinners Jesus will receive:
>   Sound the word of grace to all
> Who the heav'nly pathway leave,
>   All who linger, all who fall.
> Sing it o'er and o'er again:
> Christ receiveth sinful men.

5. *"Sometimes I am afraid that I am predestinated to be damned; if so, I can do nothing to alter my terrible case."*

No one was ever predestinated to be damned. Predestination is a precious truth of inestimable value and comfort, when rightly understood. Will you not turn to your Bible and read for yourself in the only two chapters in which this word "predestinate" or "predestinated" is found? The first is Romans 8:29-30, "For whom he did foreknow, he also did predestinate to be conformed to the image of his Son, that he might be the firstborn among many brethren. Moreover whom he did predestinate, them he also called: and whom he called, them he also justified: and whom he justified, them he also glorified."

The other chapter is Ephesians 1. In verse 5 we read, "Having predestinated us unto the adoption of children by Jesus Christ to himself, according to the good pleasure of his will." And in verse 11, it says,

"Being predestinated according to the purpose of him who worketh all things after the counsel of his own will."

You will note that there is no reference in these four verses to either heaven or hell, but to Christlikeness eventually. Nowhere are we told in Scripture that God predestinated one man to be saved and another to be lost. Men are to be saved or lost eternally because of their attitude toward the Lord Jesus Christ. "He that believeth on the Son hath everlasting life: and he that believeth not the Son shall not see life; but the wrath of God abideth on him" (John 3:36). Predestination means that some day all the redeemed shall become just like the Lord Jesus! Is not this precious? Do not try to make a bugaboo out of that which was intended to give joy and comfort to those who trust in the Saviour. Trust Him for yourself, and you will know that God has predestinated you to be fully conformed to the image of His Son.

> And is it so, I shall be like Thy Son,
> Is this the grace which He for me has won?
> Father of glory, thought beyond all thought,
> In glory to His own blest likeness brought.

6. *"I am trying to believe, but I have no assurance of salvation."*

Trying to believe whom? Would you dare speak of trying to believe the One who cannot lie? Is not this to insult God to His face? Suppose a dear friend of yours related a strange story which he declared to be a fact, would you say to him, "I will try to believe you"? Would not this be tantamount to declaring that you did not believe him at all? Do not then, I beg of you, talk of trying to believe when God has given His own testimony concerning His Son, and promised to give eternal life to all who trust Him.

You either do believe Him, or you do not. If you do not believe Him you practically make Him a liar. If you have been doing this heretofore, will you not go to Him at once and confess this great wickedness of which you have been guilty, and tell Him you will henceforth rest in simple faith upon His word? It is not a question of feeling or emotion but of "believing God and asking no questions," as that little boy put it, when asked "What is faith?"

> I do believe, I now believe,
>   That Jesus died for me,
> That on the cross He shed His blood
>   From sin to set me free.

7. *"But must I not feel different?"*

It is a remarkable fact that the word "feel" is only found once in the New Testament, and that is in Paul's sermon to the Athenians, where he rebukes them for imagining the Godhead to be like unto silver and gold, and shows that the true God is the Creator of all things, "and hath made of one blood all nations of men for to dwell on all the face of the earth, and hath determined the times before appointed, and the bounds of their habitation; that they should seek the Lord, if haply they might feel after him, and find him, though he be not far from every one of us: for in him we live, and move, and have our being; as certain also of your own poets have said, For we are also his offspring" (Acts 17:26-28). Now you find the word "feel" right in the very midst of this passage, but it has nothing to do with the gospel, but rather with the heathen groping in the dark, "if haply they might feel after God." You are not in their ignorant condition. You have heard the gospel. You know of the one living and true God. You are not told to feel anything, but to believe His record.

Then it may interest you to know that the word "feeling" is only found twice in the New Testament, and never has anything to do with the message of salvation. In Ephesians 4:19 the Spirit of God describes the state of certain unbelieving Gentiles in these words: "Who being past feeling have given themselves over unto lasciviousness, to work all uncleanness with greediness." This is what continual indulgence in sin does for people. They become insensate, "past feeling," and so conscience ceases to register, as they plunge into one excess and enormity after another.

The only other place where we read of "feeling" is in a very different connection. In Hebrews 4:15, our blessed Lord Himself is brought before us in a very precious verse: "For we have not an high priest which cannot be touched with the feeling of our infirmities; but was in all points tempted like as we are, yet without sin."

Nowhere else do we read of feeling in all the New Testament! But oh, how many times we read of believing, of faith, of trust, of confidence! Yes, these are the words for us. Ignore your feelings altogether, and tell the Lord Jesus now that you will trust Him and confess Him before men.

> Jesus, I will trust Thee,
>   Trust Thee with my soul;
> Weary, worn and helpless,
>   Thou canst make me whole.
> There is none in heaven,
>   Nor on earth like Thee;
> Thou hast died for sinners,
>   Therefore, Lord, for me.

8. *"I can see that God has done His part in the work of my salvation, but must I not do my part if I would avail myself of what He has done?"*

Have you ever heard the story of the man who was wonderfully saved and arose in a class meeting to testify to his newfound joy? His heart was filled with Christ and his lips spoke of Him and of Him only, as his Redeemer and Lord. The class leader was a legalist and said when the other had finished, "Our brother has told us what the Lord did for him, but he has forgotten to tell us what he did in order to be saved. God does His part when we do ours. Brother, did you not do your part before God saved you?" The man was on his feet in a moment and exclaimed, "I surely did do my part. I ran away from God as fast as my sins could carry me. That was my part. And God chased me till He caught me. That was His part."

Yes, you and I have all done our part, and a dreadfully sad part it was. We did all the sinning and He must do all the saving. After we are saved we can labor night and day to show our gratitude to Him for what His grace has wrought.

> I am not told to labor
>   To put away my sin;

> So foolish, weak and helpless,
>   I never could begin.
> But, blessed truth, I know it,
>   Though ruined by the fall,
> Christ for my sin has suffered,
>   Yes, Christ has done it all.

9. *"It is not exactly that I do not trust God, but I cannot be sure of myself; I am afraid even my faith is unreal."*

Faith is not the Saviour: Christ is. He is the unchanging One—"Jesus Christ, the same yesterday, and today, and forever." Faith is just the hand that lays hold of Him. You are not asked to trust yourself. The less confidence you have in yourself the better. Put all your confidence in the Lord Jesus. He is *not* unreal, and if your faith is centered in Him all will be well for time and eternity.

> Jesus, I rest in Thee,
>   In Thee myself I hide;
> Laden with sin and misery,
>   Where can I rest beside?
> 'Tis on Thy meek and lowly breast
> My burdened soul doth find its rest.

10. *"But the Bible says faith is the gift of God and that all men have not faith; perhaps it is not the will of God to give me saving faith."*

Faith is the gift of God in this sense, that only through His Word is it received. "Faith cometh by hearing, and hearing by the word of God." All men may have faith if they will: but alas, many refuse to hear the Word of God, so they are left in their unbelief. The Holy Spirit presents the Word, but one may resist His gracious influence. On the other hand, one may listen to the Word and believe it. That is faith. It is God's gift, it is true, because given through His Word.

> Not all the blood of beasts
>   On Jewish altars slain,
> Could give the guilty conscience peace,
>   Or wash away the stain.
>
> But Christ, the heav'nly Lamb,
>   Takes all our guilt away;
> A sacrifice of nobler name
>   And richer blood than they.
>
> My faith would lay her hand
>   On that dear head of Thine,
> While like a penitent I stand,
>   And there confess my sin.
>
> Believing, I rejoice
>   To see the curse remove,
> And bless the Lamb with cheerful voice,
>   And sing redeeming love.
>
> ISAAC WATTS

11. *"What troubles me is that I am not sure I have accepted Christ."*

To accept Christ is to receive Him by faith as your Lord and Saviour. But, strictly speaking, the great thing to see is that God has accepted Christ. He took our sins upon Him, died to make propitiation for them. But God has raised Him from the dead and taken Him up to glory. He has accepted Him in token of His perfect satisfaction in His work. Believing this, the soul enters into peace. I simply rest in God's thoughts about His Son.

Peace with God is Christ in glory,
  God is light and God is love;
Jesus died to tell the story,
  Foes to bring to God above.

12. *"Sometimes I believe I have trusted Jesus and am justified before God, but I cannot forget my sins; they come before me night and day. Surely, if I were really forgiven I could forget the past."*

Ah, dear troubled one, the closer you get to Christ, and the more deeply you repent of your sins, the more you will abhor yourself for ever committing them. But let your comfort be in this blessed thought—God has forgotten them! He says, "Their sins and iniquities will I remember no more." So when they come before your mind to trouble and distress you, just rest in the fact that God has forgotten them, and will never bring them up again. Christ has settled for all of those sins. Believe it and be at peace.

Settled forever, sin's tremendous claim,
  Glory to Jesus, blessed be His name;
No part-way measures doth His grace provide,
  Finished the work, when Christ the Saviour died.

13. *"I often come to the point of deciding for Christ, then I draw back because I am afraid I cannot hold out."*

If it were a matter of your own ability to hold out, you might well fear. You have no power in yourself that will enable you to hold out. But the moment you fully trust the Lord Jesus you are born again. Then the Holy Spirit comes in to dwell in your heart and to be the power of the new life. He will enable you to resist temptation and to live to the glory of

God. "It is God which worketh in you both to will and to do of his good pleasure." Do not count on self at all. Let Him have His way. He will lead you on in triumph as you surrender to Him.

> Safe in the Lord, without a doubt,
>   By virtue of the blood:
> For nothing can destroy the life
>   That's hid with Christ in God!

14. *"But must I not hold on to the end if I would be saved at last?"*

May I, without irreverence, venture to recast a Bible story? If the account of Noah and the flood went something like this, what would you think of it? Suppose that after the ark was completed God said unto Noah, "Now, get eight great spikes of iron and drive them into the side of the ark." And Noah procured the spikes and did as he was bidden. Then the word came unto him, "Come thou and all thy house and hang on to these spikes." And Noah and his wife, and the three sons and their wives, each held onto a spike. And the rains descended and the flood came, and as the ark was borne up on the waters their muscles were strained to the utmost as they clung to the spikes. Imagine God saying to them, "If you hang on till the deluge is over you will be saved!" Can you even think of such a thing as anyone of them going safely through?

But oh, how different the simple Bible story. "And the LORD said unto Noah, Come thou and all thy house into the ark." Ah, that is a very different thing than holding on! Inside the ark they were safe as long as the ark endured the storm. And every believer is in Christ and is as safe as God can make him. Look away then from all self-effort and trust Him alone. Rest in the ark and rejoice in God's great salvation.

And be sure to remember that it is Christ who holds you, not you who hold Him. He has said, "I will never leave thee, nor forsake thee." "For if, when we were enemies, we were reconciled to God by the death of his Son, much more, being reconciled, we shall be saved by his life" (Rom. 5:10). He who died for you, now lives at God's right hand to keep you, and the Father sees you in Him. "He hath made us accepted in the beloved." Could anything be more sure?

> The work which His goodness began,
> The arm of His strength will complete;
> His promise is Yea and Amen,
> And never was forfeited yet.

15. *"Must I not strive, if I would enter in at the strait gate? It seems to me just believing is too easy a way."*

Our Lord's words may well give us pause. They were never intended, however, to make us feel that a hard struggle was necessary in order to be saved. But He would have us understand that no one will ever be saved who is not in earnest. The great majority of people drift aimlessly and carelessly on, passing heedlessly by the gate to life, intent only on gratifying their carnal and worldly desires. He who would be saved must arouse himself to the supreme importance of spiritual things. He must put first things first. In this sense he strives to enter in at the strait gate.

He will be like Bunyan's pilgrim who, when awakened to his danger and realizing the dreadful burden of sin, refused to heed the pleadings of his old companions, and putting his fingers in his ears, cried, "Life, life, eternal life!" as he fled from the City of Destruction. You, too, must determine that nothing shall be allowed to interfere with the settlement of the great matter of the salvation of your soul.

But you do not have to strive with God to save you. He is waiting to do that very thing. Yea, and He will do it for you the moment you cease from all self-effort and put your trust in Christ. To strive to enter in is to be determined that nothing shall keep you from accepting the gracious invitation of the Lord Jesus, who bids you come to Him in all your need and guilt, that He may fit you for heaven's glory by cleansing you from every stain. Do not on any account be turned away from this, but brushing every barrier aside, yield your heart to the Saviour now.

> He tells me words whereby I'm saved,
>   He points to something done,
> Accomplished on Mount Calvary
>   By His beloved Son;
> In which no works of mine have place,
> Else grace with works were no more grace.

16. *"Do I not have to wait God's time? I can do nothing about it until He is ready to save me."*

But God's time is now. He plainly tells us, "Behold, now is the accepted time; behold, now is the day of salvation." You need not wait another moment. He will never be any more ready to save you than He is at the very instant you are reading these words, and you will never be more fit to come to Him than at this very moment. Every day you wait you are adding to the terrible list of your sins. Every hour you continue to reject Him you are increasing your guilt by refusing to receive His blessed Son. Every moment you stay away from Him you are sinning against His love. Why not close up the present evil record by prostrating yourself before Him now, and owning your need, accept the gift of God, which is eternal life?

> I was waiting once for pardon,
>   I was hoping to be saved;
> Waiting, though my heart would harden,
>   Hoping danger might be braved.
> Till by God's own truth confounded,
>   I, a sinner, stood confessed;
> Richly then His grace abounded,
>   Jesus gave me perfect rest.

17. *"I really want to come to Jesus, but I do not seem to know how to do so."*

It is strange how we stumble over the very simplicity of the gospel invitation. Christ Jesus is a living, loving, divinely human Personality—as truly as when He was here on earth. It is He Himself who bids us come. Do you know what it is to stay away? Then surely you need have no difficulty in doing the very opposite! Lift your heart to Him in prayer. Tell Him that you are the sinner for whom He died, and that now you accept His gracious invitation to "Come, for all things are now ready." Then believe that He receives you, for He said He would and He always keeps His word.

You may have heard the story of Charlotte Elliot, the hymn writer. As a young woman she was troubled and anxious about her soul, but very reticent when it came to seeking help from others. But a French pastor, who was visiting her father, put the question directly to her, "Have you come to Jesus?" She replied, "I want to come, but I do not know how." He simply answered, "Come just as you are." She fled to her room in tears and later emerged a saved soul. She wrote the well-known lines quoted below as the expression of her own coming. Will you not make them yours?

> Just as I am, without one plea,
> But that Thy blood was shed for me,
> And that Thou bidd'st me come to Thee,
>   O Lamb of God! I come, I come!
>
> Just as I am, Thy love unknown
> Hath broken ev'ry barrier down;
> Now to be Thine, yea, Thine alone,
>   O Lamb of God! I come, I come!

18. *"Must I not pray through until I get the witness that I am saved?"*

Nowhere in the Bible are people told they must pray to be saved. It is true that the natural expression of an awakened and anxious soul is prayer. But there is no such thing in Scripture as "praying through" in order to be saved. What is required is that the convicted sinner believe the gospel. Suppose you went home tired and hungry, and said to your wife, "Will you please let me have supper as early as possible?" She complies at once and sets the table, calling you to come and partake of what she has provided. Instead of doing so, you plead long and earnestly, literally begging for food. What would she think of you?

And what does God think when He has spread the gospel feast for starving sinners and invited all to "come and dine," but instead of obeying His voice, men fall on their knees and beg and plead for His mercy and grace, and do not accept His invitation and feast on the living bread provided for their salvation.

The witness of the Spirit is only enjoyed by those who thus take Him at His word. The believer has received the witness *to* him as given in the Word of God (Heb. 10:15). He has the witness *in* himself because the truth has been received into his heart (I John 5:10). He enjoys the Spirit's witnessing *with* his spirit, when, upon believing, the Holy Spirit comes to dwell within (Rom. 8:16). The witness is not a happy feeling. It is the testimony that the Spirit gives through the Word. That this testimony believed brings joy and gladness goes without question. I do not know I am saved because I feel happy. But I feel happy because I know I am saved. An old evangelist I knew as a boy often used to say, "Believing is the root; feeling is the fruit." This expresses it well.

> O the peace my Saviour gives,
>   Peace I never knew before;
> And the way has brighter grown,
>   Since I've learned to trust Him more.

19. *"Sometimes I fear that I have sinned away my day of grace, for though I have been seeking the*

Lord for a long time, I do not seem to find Him."

No one has sinned away his day of grace who has any desire to be saved. That desire is divinely implanted. If you are seeking after God it is because He is seeking after you. But, what, after all, do you really mean when you talk of seeking the Lord and being unable to find Him? He is not hiding Himself. He has come in love to sinners as the good Shepherd seeking the lost sheep.

A little boy was asked one day, "My lad, have you found Jesus?" He looked up in amazement and replied, "Why, sir, I didn't know He was lost; but I was, and He found me." A wonderful confession surely!

In Old Testament times God said through the prophet, "Seek ye the LORD while he may be found, call ye upon him while he is near"; and there is a sense in which these words are still applicable. But they do not convey the full truth of the gospel. Jesus said, "The Son of man is come to seek and to save that which was lost" (Luke 19:10). Are you lost? Then He is looking for you. "Stand still, and see the salvation of the Lord." Stop right where you are and lift your heart to Him as a repentant sinner, and you will find He is waiting and ready to receive you.

And as to sinning away your day of grace, has He not said, "Whosoever will may come"? Are you not included in that great word "whosoever"? Unless you can prove that it does not take you in, you are still where the grace of God can reach you. Do not listen to the lying voice of the enemy of your soul, who tells you that your case is hopeless, but heed the gentle invitation of Him who is the way, the truth, and the life, as He bids you now believe on His name.

> And if I now would seek Him,
> In love He sought for me,
> When far from Him I wandered
> In sin and misery;
> He oped my ears and bade me
> To listen to His call;
> He sought me and He found me—
> Yes, Christ has done it all.

20. *"But how can I be sure that my faith is strong enough to save my soul?"*

It is not faith that saves the soul. It is the One whom God has set forth as the object of faith. It is true we are justified by faith instrumentally, but actually we are justified by His blood. The weakest faith in Jesus saves. The strongest faith in self, or in good works, or in the church, or in its ordinances leaves you lost and undone still.

James Parker of Plainfield, New Jersey, was visiting in a hospital, when a nurse indicated a bed surrounded with white screens, and whispered, "The poor man is dying. The priest has been here and administered the last sacrament. He cannot live long." Mr. Parker begged to go inside the screen, and permission was granted. As he looked down upon the dying man he observed a crucifix on his bosom. He stooped over and lifted it up. The sick man lifted his eyes and looked distressed. "Put it back," he whispered, "I want to die with it on my breast." The visitor pointed to the figure pictured on the cross, and said fervently, "He's a wonderful Saviour!"

"Yes, yes, I love the crucifix. Put it back, please. I hope it will help me to die well."

"Not the crucifix," was the reply, "but the One who died on the cross, the Lord Jesus, He died to save you."

The man looked bewildered, then his face brightened: "Oh, I see, not the crucifix but the One who died. He died for me. I see, sir, I see. I never understood it before."

It was evident that faith had sprung up in his soul. Mr. Parker replaced the crucifix, offered a brief prayer, and left. In a few minutes he observed the body being wheeled out of the ward.

Telling me of it later, he exclaimed, "I know that God thinks so much of the work of His Son that He will have everyone in heaven who will give Him any excuse for taking them there!" It is blessedly true. Faith's look at the Crucified saves, even though it be faith of the feeblest kind.

> There is life in a look at the Crucified One,
>   There is life at this moment for thee;
> Then look, sinner, look unto Him and be saved,
>   Unto Him who was nailed to the tree.

21. *"But must I not keep the law in order to be saved?"*

Keep the law! Why you have already violated those sacred precepts times without number. Go carefully over the Ten Commandments; which of them have you not broken, either literally or in spirit? Take them one by one, and face them squarely and honestly in the presence of the God who gave them, and who said,

"The man that doeth them shall live in them"; but who also declared, "Cursed is every one that continueth not in all things which are written in the book of the law to do them." Let us consider them seriously:

a. "Thou shalt have no other gods before me."

He is downright exclusive! He must be the one object of worship! But have you given Him this place in your life? Have not many other gods shared your love and veneration? We are commanded to love the Lord our God with all the heart, mind, soul, and strength. Have you ever risen to this? If not, plead guilty on count one, and pass on to the next.

b. "Thou shalt not make unto thee any graven image. . . . Thou shalt not bow down thyself to them, nor serve them."

Of gross idolatry, involving the actual adoration of images you may never have been guilty; but we read in Scripture of some who set up idols in their hearts. And these are as obnoxious to God as idols of wood, or stone, or metal. What are some of their names? Self, Wealth, Fame, Pleasure, and many more. The devotees of these false gods are as truly idolaters as the heathen who bow down to carved and molten symbols. Are you guilty of such false worship? If so, bow in humiliation before the one true and living God, and cry again, "Guilty."

c. "Thou shalt not take the name of the LORD thy God in vain."

How widespread is the wicked practice of profanity! "Swear not at all" is the command of Holy Scripture. Yet how few there are who have not sinned along this line. Remember, it is not always necessary to use vile, wicked language to profane the name of the Lord. When that name is used carelessly, lightly, without due respect and reverence, this commandment is broken just as truly as when coupled with oaths and cursing. And many a one swears in thought whose lips have never been sullied by cursing. Can you honestly face this third commandment and cry, "Not guilty"?

d. "Remember the sabbath day, to keep it holy."

God claims one-seventh of man's time. He gives six days for useful labor and lawful pleasure. He demands that one day be set aside for Himself. "The sabbath was made for man, not man for the sabbath." But what base ingratitude have we manifested here! The disregard for God's holy day is but an evidence of the rebellion of the human heart against all divine authority. What can you say for yourself as to this? Are you guilty or not guilty? Answer as at the bar of eternal justice.

e. "Honor thy father and thy mother."

One of the outstanding sins of the last days is "disobedience to parents." Self-will is everywhere apparent. Where is the child that has always been dutiful and obedient? Lack of filial regard is scarcely considered a sin anymore. But He who on earth was subject to His mother and His foster-father is our example. How far short we have come of the perfection seen in Him! Be absolutely honest with yourself and with God. If you have ever been a disobedient, willful child, do not attempt to justify your wrongdoing, but take the penitent sinner's place and own your guilt.

f. "Thou shalt not kill."

Your hand may never have been stained with human blood. But what of that passage in the first epistle of John, "Whosoever hateth his brother is a murderer." Judged by this high and holy standard, who is beyond condemnation here?

g. "Thou shalt not commit adultery."

Many there are who have kept themselves physically pure from this gross sin, but how few have always been pure in thought; and the Lord Jesus told us that an unchaste look is adultery in the sight of God. This raises a standard that few, if any, have been able to wholly live up to. If uncleanness in act or in thought has ever soiled your soul, do not try to excuse it, as do the psychologists of our degenerate times, but bow with the woman of the seventh chapter of Luke and the other woman of the eighth chapter of John at the feet of Jesus, own your guilt, and hear Him say, "Thy sins are forgiven. Neither do I condemn thee: go, and sin no more."

h. "Thou shalt not steal."

We are apt to think of stealing as involving large sums of money, or the purloining of valuable goods. But he is as really a thief who steals a trifle, as he who burglarizes a house or embezzles a million. Who is entirely guiltless of appropriating what was not rightfully his?

i. "Thou shalt not bear false witness."

Have your lips never been stained with a lie? "The wicked," we are told, "go astray as soon as they are born, speaking lies." It has often been noted that all children need to be taught to speak the truth. None ever need lessons in lying, for "out of the abundance of the heart the mouth speaketh." And "the heart is deceitful above all things." Therefore, deceitful lips and practices. Whoever dares to say, "I am not guilty" on this count is but adding another lie to the many yet to be answered for.

j. "Thou shalt not covet."

This was the prohibition that convicted self-righteous Saul of Tarsus of his sinfulness. He who could claim that as to outward observances he was guiltless of violations, found himself a slave to desires for what God had withheld from him, and so "the commandment which was ordained to life," he found "to be unto death." For sin, taking occasion by the commandment, wrought in him all manner of concupiscence (covetousness, lust, evil desire) and thus he realized he was a helpless slave, unable to break the chains that bound him. Do you find yourself in the same state? Then let the voice of the law have its way. Own its authority and admit you are under condemnation.

Even One Offense Means Guilt

Now possibly you find, by careful examination, that you are not guilty on every count of these ten words. But remember what the Holy Spirit has told us in James 2:8-11: "If ye fulfil the royal law according to the scripture, Thou shalt love thy neighbor as thyself, ye do well: but if ye have respect to persons, ye commit sin, and are convinced of the law as transgressors. For whosoever shall keep the whole law, and yet offend in one point, he is guilty of all. For he that said, Do not commit adultery, said also, Do not kill.

Now if thou commit no adultery, yet if thou kill, thou art become a transgressor of the law."

It has often been remarked that a chain is no stronger than its weakest link. Suppose you were suspended over a precipice by a chain of ten links. How many would need to snap before you would drop into the abyss below? And so, if you are guilty of the violation of one of the commandments, you are condemned by the law and therefore under its curse.

The law of God was never given to save men. It was given to magnify sin, to make it exceedingly sinful, to give it the specific character of transgression. "Therefore by the deeds of the law there shall no man be justified in his sight: for by the law is the knowledge of sin" (Rom. 3:20). But, blessed be God, "Christ hath redeemed us from the curse of the law, being made a curse for us: for it is written, Cursed is every one that hangeth on a tree" (Gal. 3:13). He became man, and was born under the law. He obeyed that law perfectly, and was not subject to its penalty. But He went to the cross and endured its curse for us, that we who trust Him might be forever free from its just condemnation. "He that believeth on him is not condemned: but he that believeth not is condemned already, because he hath not believed in the name of the only begotten Son of God" (John 3:18). "There is therefore now no condemnation to those who are in Christ Jesus" (Rom. 8:1).

> Free from the law, oh, happy condition,
> Jesus hath bled, and there is remission;

Curs'd by the law and bruised by the fall,
Christ hath redeemed us once for all.

22. *"But must I not first make restitution for all the
wrongs I have done to other people before I
can come to Christ and be forgiven?"*

It is good that you are exercised as to wrongs done
to others, but nowhere in the Word are we told we
must make restitution first, though after we are saved
we should certainly seek to do all in our power to
straighten up any crooked things involving the rights
of other people. It is to those already saved that the
apostle writes, "Let him that stole steal no more: but
rather let him labor, working with his hands the thing
which is good, that he may have to give to him that
needeth" (Eph. 4:28).

Consider the repentant thief on the cross. Surely
he had been guilty of wronging many of his fellows!
Yet the moment he turned in faith to Jesus he was
saved. In the very nature of the case he could not
make restitution to anyone for any crime committed.
His hands and feet were nailed to the cross. It was
not possible for him to do one thing to repair the
many wrongs he had done. But through the merits of
the holy Sufferer on that central cross, he was fully
and freely pardoned and fitted for paradise. Had he
been permitted to live, and to come down from that
scaffold, undoubtedly he would have spent his life
seeking to show the reality of his repentance, and
wherever possible to make restitution for offences
committed. But he was saved altogether apart from
this; and that on the ground of the propitiatory work
of the Lord Jesus Christ.

You may be saved in the very same way. Then as a new man in Christ, you can prove your love to Him by striving to live unselfishly and devotedly to His glory. And if you are able to put wrongs right, as between man and man, you will in so doing not only find joy yourself, but you will be a witness to others of the power of saving grace. But all such efforts to clean up the past will have nothing whatever to do with the salvation of your soul. You cannot even help God to save you. It is Christ's work alone that counts.

> Cast your deadly doing down,
>   Down at Jesus' feet;
> Stand in Him, in Him alone,
>   Gloriously complete.

23. *"I humbly hope that I am a Christian, but I dare not be too sure. I cannot see how anyone can be certain until after the day of judgment."*

But the day of judgment will be too late! If this matter is not settled before that great assize, you will then be irrevocably lost. Perhaps you are laboring under a misapprehension of what that judgment of the great white throne is for, and who is to be judged at that time. It will be the judgment of sinners, when all who have lived and died out of Christ will be judged according to their works. Christians will not stand there for judgment. Concerning them our Lord has said (John 5:24): "Verily, verily, I say unto you, He that heareth my word, and believeth on him that sent me, hath everlasting life, and shall not come into condemnation; but is passed from death unto life."

I like the Douay translation of this verse, which

is confirmed by our Revised Version. It changes "shall not come into condemnation" into "cometh not into judgment." Here is a glorious truth revealed! The believer in the Lord Jesus will never have to be judged for his sins because Christ has been judged for them already. On account of this God justifies freely and completely all who receive His Son in faith as their Saviour. Look again at the verse quoted above. Notice that all who hear His Word and believe in Him have everlasting life. It is present possession. Therefore it is really unbelief that would lead one to say, "I hope I have eternal life because I believe in Jesus." Do not speak of humility when you are doubting God. Take Him at His word and know beyond all question that eternal life is yours.

> Though all unworthy, yet I will not doubt,
> For him that cometh He will not cast out;
> He that believeth, oh, the good news shout,
> Hath everlasting life.

24. *"Must I not first be baptized before I can know that I am saved?"*

It is right and proper that you should be baptized. But baptism cannot effect the salvation of the soul. It is, as Peter tells us, a figure of salvation, just as was the deliverance of Noah in the ark of old. But we are told distinctly, "By grace are ye saved through faith; and that not of yourselves: it is the gift of God" (Eph. 2:8). To the inquiring jailer at Philippi, who asked the definite question, "What must I do to be saved?" there came as definite an answer, "Believe on the Lord Jesus Christ, and thou shalt be saved." (See Acts 16.) Baptism followed believing. It was the God-ordained way of confessing Christ as Saviour and Lord. Many have been saved who could not possibly be baptized. Consider again the case of the penitent thief, and be assured that God has never had two ways of saving sinners. The same grace that saved him will save you, when you trust in Jesus, whose blood alone cleanses from all sin.

There are a number of passages relating to baptism that may seem a little confusing. But rest your soul on the clear, definite statement concerning salvation by grace and as you study your Bible the perplexing portions will become clearer under the Holy Spirit's guidance. It is Christ's baptism of judgment that is the basis of our deliverance from death.

> Lord Jesus, we remember
>   The travail of Thy soul;
> When in Thy love's deep pity
>   The waves did o'er Thee roll.
> Baptized in death's dark waters,
>   For us Thy blood was shed;
> For us Thou Lord of glory
>   Wast numbered with the dead.

25. *"If I could only be sure I was in the right church, I would feel secure; but there are so many different churches that I get all confused and upset."*

The church is not the ark of safety. The church is the aggregate of all who believe in the Lord Jesus and who have therefore been baptized by the Holy Spirit into one body. This is not a mere organization, however ancient and venerable. If you *were* sure you were in the right church (some earthly organization), and trusted in that for salvation, you would be forever lost! Your trust must be in the Head of the church, the risen Christ. He is the only Saviour. All ecclesiastical pretention is vain and to rest in any kind of church membership is an empty deception. Christ alone is the ark that will carry you safely through all the storms of judgment. No matter what denomination you turn to, you will never find salvation in allying yourself with it, but when you come to Jesus, you are then prepared to enjoy fellowship with His people.

> I love Thy kingdom, Lord,
>   The house of Thine abode,
> The Church our blest Redeemer saved
>   With His own precious blood.

26. *"I believe that Jesus died for me, but I am afraid to say I am saved, for I know I do not love God as much as I should."*

I question if anyone loves Him as He ought to be loved. But it is a grave mistake to be looking in your own heart for love. Rather rejoice in the amazing love of God for you as expressed in the cross of Christ, and in all His care for you through the years. We say sometimes that love begets love. This is very true in regard to love for God. As you are occupied with His love, your own heart will respond to it and you will be able to say, "We love him, because he first loved us." Looking into your own heart for a ground of confidence is like casting the anchor in the hold of a ship. Cast it outside and let it go down, down, down into the great, tossing ocean of strife and trouble, until it grips the rock itself. Christ alone is the rock, and He is the manifestation of the infinite love of God for sinners.

The following lines are of uncertain authorship, but they are most blessedly true:

> Could we with ink the ocean fill,
> Were the world of parchment made,
> Were every blade of grass a quill,
> And every man a scribe by trade,
>   To write the love
>   Of God above
> Would drain that ocean dry;
>   Nor would the scroll
>   Contain the whole,
> Though stretched from sky to sky!

27. *"At times I feel assured that all is well, but at other times I tremble, fearing that I am mistaken."*

Mistaken about what? If you believe that Jesus died for you and rose again, there can be no mistake about that. If you have taken Him at His word, and have come to Him for peace and pardon, there can be no mistake about that. If you have opened your heart to Him, you can be certain He has come in to abide, for He has told you He would, and there can be no mistake about that. Your trembling does not alter these basic facts.

A story is told of a vessel that was wrecked one stormy night by crashing on the rocks off the coast of Cornwall. All hands perished but one lone Irish lad, who was hurled by the waves upon the jagged slopes of a great towering ledge, where he managed to find a place of refuge. In the morning, watchers on the beach spied him through their glasses, and a boat was launched and rowed out to where he clung. Almost dead with cold and exposure, he was tenderly lifted into the boat and brought ashore. After restoratives were applied, he was asked, "Lad, didn't ye tremble out there on the rock in all that storm?" He replied brightly in his Irish way, "Trimble? Sure and I trimbled. But do you know, the rock never trimbled wanct all night." If you have trusted Christ you are on the rock. While you may tremble, that does not invalidate God's salvation. The rock remains firm and secure. Look away from self altogether and rely solely upon the Word of God.

> When darkness veils His lovely face,
> I rest on His unchanging grace;
> In ev'ry high and stormy gale,
> My anchor holds within the veil.
> On Christ, the solid Rock, I stand,
> All other ground is sinking sand.

28. *"There have been times when I had very definite assurance of my salvation, and then I have lost it again. Why do these periods of darkness come?"*

There may be various reasons for these periods of darkness. The greatest saints have at times known the same experiences. They may possibly be accounted for by great mental weariness and physical weakness. The adversary of our souls is always ready to take advantage of such conditions, and ever seeks to make us forget the clear, definite promises of God on which we have rested when well and strong.

There is an authentic story told of an aged minister, who had preached the gospel in clearness and power during all his public life, but who, when he was suffering at times, found himself greatly beset by doubt and uncertainty. Mentioning the matter to his wife, she drew his attention to John 5:24. As he read the precious words again, "Verily, verily, I say unto you, He that heareth my word, and believeth on him that sent me, hath everlasting life, and shall not come into condemnation; but is passed from death unto life," he burst into a joyous laugh, and said, "How strange that I should ever forget words like these, when I have preached on them myself for years."

Sometime later the wife came into the room and found her aged husband leaning over the side of the bed, holding the open Bible beneath his couch. She exclaimed, "Whatever are you doing?" He answered, "Satan has been after me again and as he is the prince of darkness, I took it that he would be in the darkest place in the room, which is under the bed, and so I was just showing him John 5:24, and the moment he saw it he ceased to trouble me."

We can quite understand the mental weakness that the story suggests, but the principle is blessedly true. When the adversary of your soul comes against you seeking to destroy your confidence, show him what God has said.

But there may be other reasons which account for the loss of that blessed assurance you once enjoyed. The Apostle Peter suggests such in his second epistle, chapter 1, verse 9. In the previous verses he has been stressing the importance of spiritual growth, and the believer is instructed to be diligent in adding to his faith virtue, and to virtue knowledge, and to knowledge self-control, and to self-control patience, and to patience godliness, and to godliness brotherly kindness and to brotherly kindness love; and then he can be sure that if these things are in him and abound, he will not be idle nor unfruitful in the knowledge of our Lord Jesus Christ.

But, on the other hand, if the believer is neglectful of these things, he cannot expect the divine blessing to rest upon him; and so we are told, "He that lacketh these things is blind, and cannot see afar off, and hath forgotten that he was purged from his old sins." There is something very solemn here. Notice, he was purged from his old sins, but through indolence and carelessness he has lost the assurance of this. The blessedness of bygone days has faded from his memory.

The Christian life is never static. One must either grow in grace, or there will be backsliding and deterioration. "The backslider in heart shall be filled with his own ways" (Prov. 14:14). He who does not go on with God, but allows himself to drift, is almost sure to lose the joy of his salvation. Examine yourself as to this matter, and if you find that you have been careless in regard to the study of your Bible, careless as to your prayer life, careless as to the proper use of the means of grace, confess all this to God and give diligence to walk with Him in days to come, that you may develop a stronger Christian character.

Last of all, let me remind you that any known sin condoned in your life will rob you of the joy and assurance of your salvation. "If I regard iniquity in my heart, the LORD will not hear me." Many a one who has gone on happily with Christ for sometime, has later toyed with sin and become ensnared and entrapped into something that has so grieved the Spirit of God that he has lost his sense of acceptance in Christ. See to it that there is no unconfessed sin in your life. Be sure that you are not tolerating any secret sin which is draining you of spiritual power and hindering your communion with God.

Worldliness, carnal indulgence of any kind, unfaithfulness as to your Christian responsibilities, unseemly levity, the harboring of malice or ill-will toward others —all or any of these things are calculated to destroy your sense of assurance. If guilty of any of them, face things honestly in the presence of God, remembering that He has said, "If we confess our sins, he is faithful and just to forgive us our sins, and to cleanse us from all unrighteousness."

Do not accept the suggestion of the tempter that you are powerless to break away from evil habits. Remember it is not a question of your own power, but when you honestly repent of the wrongdoing and turn to the Lord for divine help to overcome your besetting sin, He will undertake for you. As you reckon yourself to be dead indeed unto sin, but alive unto God through Jesus Christ our Lord, the Holy Spirit will work in and through you, causing you to triumph over tendencies toward evil, and enabling you to live victoriously to the glory of the God who has saved you.

2

CONCLUDING WORDS OF COUNSEL

Now, I REALIZE that your particular difficulty may not have been touched at all in the preceding pages. But whatever it is that keeps you from the positive assurance that your soul is saved, I beg of you not to give up in despair and conclude that such knowledge is not for you. For whatever your condition of mind, whatever your trouble of conscience, whatever your particular besetment may be, there is that in God's holy Word which is designed to exactly meet your case.

Will you not definitely settle it with God that you will take the Lord Jesus Christ as your own personal Saviour, and then, in dependence upon the Holy Spirit, search the Scriptures daily, reading prayerfully and thoughtfully, and look up to God Himself for all needed enlightenment? "The meek will he guide in judgment: and the meek will he teach his way." Again, He says, "To this man will I look, even to him that is poor and of a contrite spirit, and trembleth at my word."

Our blessed Lord has declared that if one is willing to do the will of God, he shall know of the doctrine. All that is needed is to take the place of a lost sinner, in humility of mind and contrition of heart, counting upon God who is not willing that any should perish to reveal His mind to you through the written Word, thus leading on to the assurance of peace with God through Jesus Christ.

But, on the other hand, do not be neglectful of the means of grace He has put at your disposal. If you are so located that you can attend upon the ministry of the Word, go as often as you can to hear the gospel proclaimed, for when the world by its wisdom knew not God, "it pleased God by the foolishness of preaching to save them that believe." Frequent, too, the place of prayer, and be ready to consult with others who give evidence of knowing and enjoying what you are seeking for. It was when Lydia was at the place of prayer that Paul was sent to explain the way of life, and the Lord opened her heart to receive it. She was earnestly seeking in accordance with all the light she had, and the Lord saw to it that more light came as she followed the gleam.

Another thing is very important for anyone desiring divine illumination: Put out of your life every known sin, so far as it is in your power to do so, and avoid all that would tend to defile your mind and heart. David said, "If I regard iniquity in my heart, the LORD will not hear me." If you continue to associate needlessly with the ungodly, or if you participate in worldly pleasures, all of which have a tendency to harden the conscience, you cannot expect to get help from the Spirit of God, who is grieved by all such frivolities.

Do not waste precious time on trashy and unclean literature. Read only what is uplifting and inspiring.

Give the first place to your Bible and avail yourself of good books as you are able to obtain them, books that edify and make eternal things more real. It is folly to expect the assurance of salvation and yet neglect the means that God has ordained for making known the riches of His grace.

Moody Press, a ministry of the Moody Bible Institute, is designed for education, evangelization and edification. If we may assist you in knowing more about Christ and the Christian life, please write us without obligation to: Moody Press, c/o MLM, Chicago, Illinois 60610.

Printed in the United States of America

FULL ASSURANCE

H. A. Ironside

Doubts. They creep up slowly, quietly. They nag at us. *I don't feel good enough for God. I'm too great a sinner to be saved. Shouldn't I feel different? If my sins are forgiven, why can't I forget them?*

With straightforward answers, H. A. Ironside helps us see clearly that we need not have these or any other doubts about our salvation. We have eternal assurance of our settled peace with God. Faith, hope, and understanding are guaranteed to us.

Don't wait any longer. Read this book now and be sure.

0125MP

DOCTRINE   ISBN: 0-8024-2896-7